VIEWS

of MICHIGAN

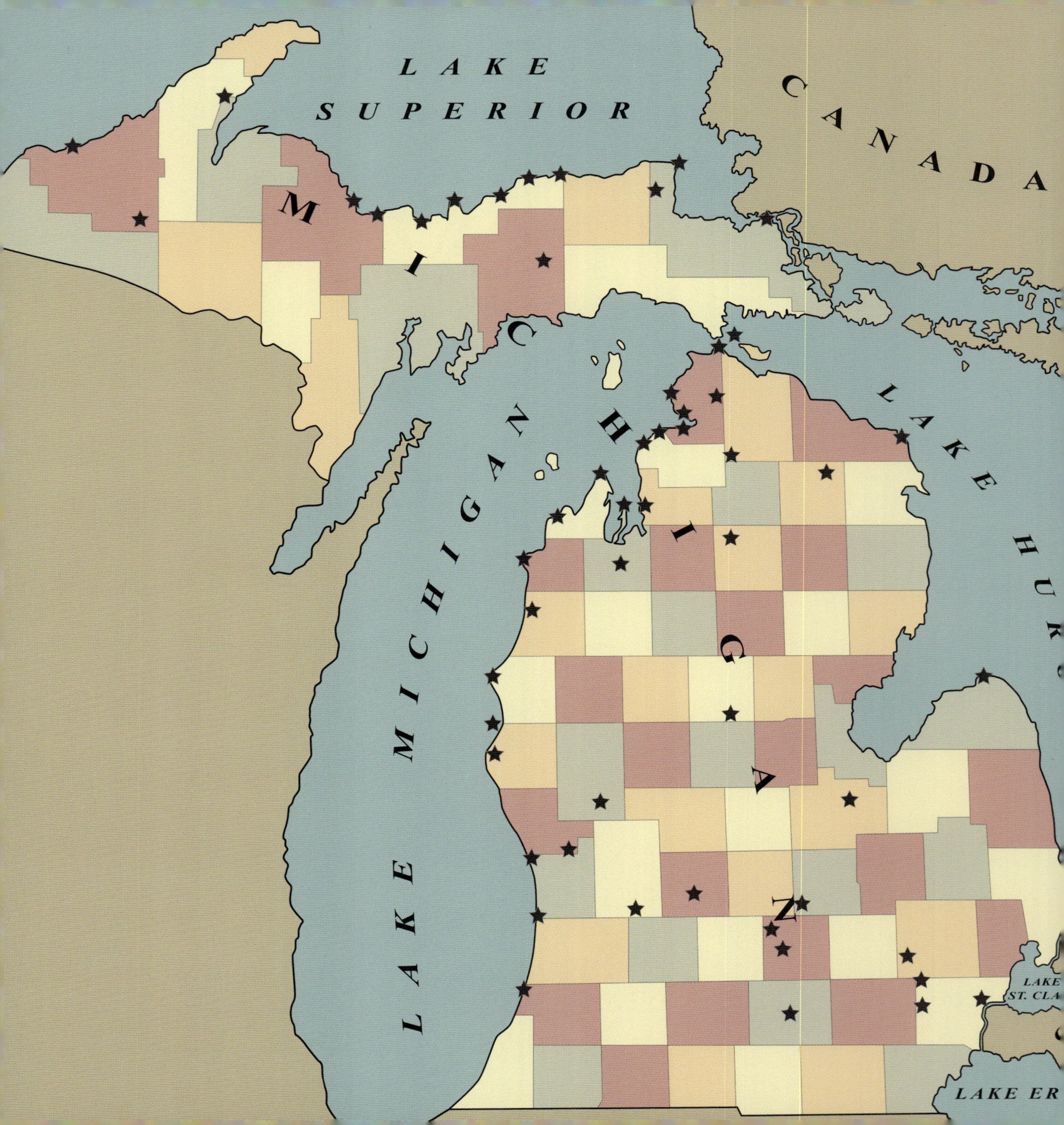

LAKE SUPERIOR
CANADA
MICHIGAN
LAKE MICHIGAN
LAKE HUR
LAKE ST. CLA
LAKE ER

VIEWS

of MICHIGAN

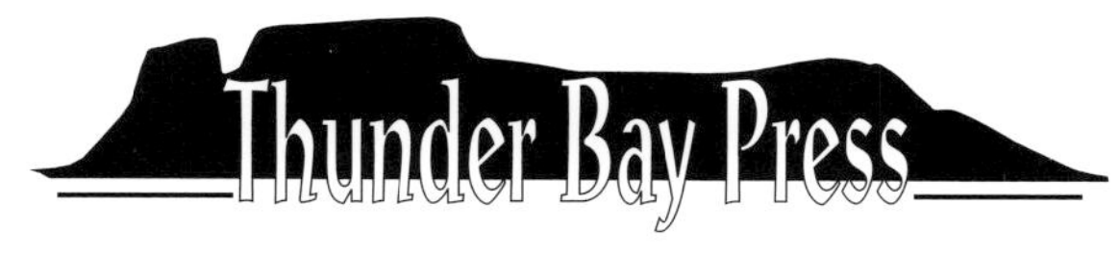

Holt, MI

Published 2013 by
Thunder Bay Press
2325 Jarco Drive
Holt, MI 48842

ISBN: 978-1-933272-35-1

Library of Congress Control Number: 2013933415

First Edition 2013

17 16 15 14 13 1 2 3 4 5

Cover image: Grand Haven Pier and Lighthouse by Alan L. Jones.

Book and cover design, Map of Michigan by Julie Taylor.
Photographs compiled by Sam Speigel, Julie Taylor, Amelia Turkette, and Sara Wells Speigel.

"Hoary Puccoon" by Joyce Benvenuto. Originally published in the *Green River Review*, Saginaw Valley State College, 1982, Michigan Poets. Published in *A Grand River*, a collection of poems by Joyce Benvenuto, Thunder Bay Press, 2012.

Printed in the United States of America by Versa Press | East Peoria, Illinois

Si Quaeris Peninsulam Amoenam
Circumspice

If you seek a pleasant peninsula,
look about you.

—Michigan State Motto

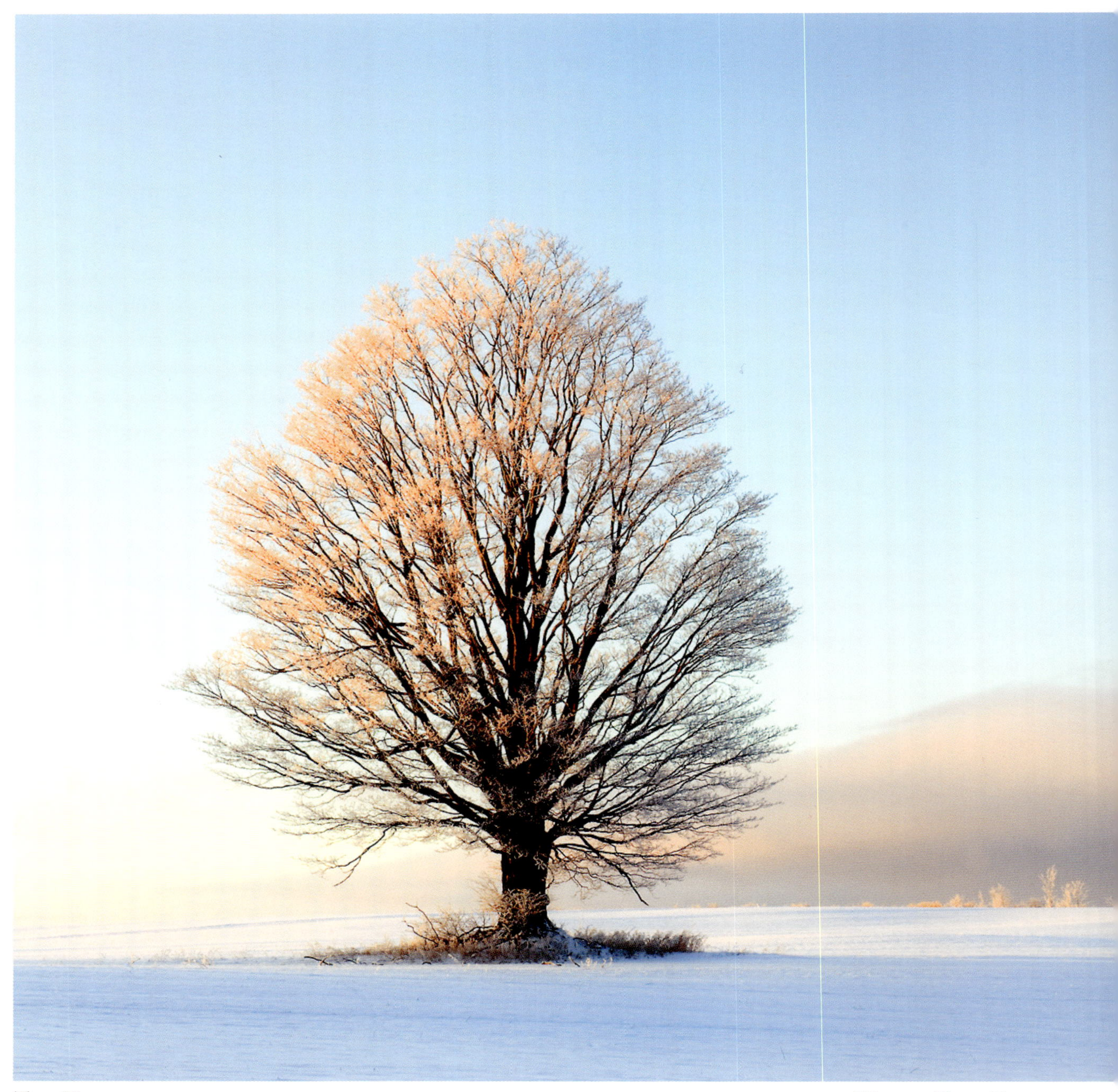

Tom Haxby — Winter Tree, Kingsley

THE MANY MICHIGANS

JERRY DENNIS

When my brother and I were kids we threw fits every time our parents tried taking us on vacation. We lived on the shore of a lake in northwest lower Michigan, with a dock and boats and a neighbor's diving raft we could use any time we wanted in the summer, and snowmobiles and skis and an ice-shanty we could use in the winter. Everything we wanted was at home on Long Lake and in the woods and fields across the road. Why would we ever leave paradise?

But our parents were determined to show us that the world consisted of more than our little corner of it, so they dragged us along to Tiger Stadium and Greenfield Village in Detroit, to visit relatives who worked in the auto plants in Flint, to walk Lake Michigan beaches on the west shore of the Lower Peninsula and Lake Superior beaches on the north shore of the Upper Peninsula. We camped, fished, hunted, gathered mushrooms, collected fossils, identified birds and wildflowers, explored museums and ghost towns. Gradually we began to realize that Michigan was one of the great and bountiful places in North America and that a person could spend a lifetime there and never see it all.

For of course Michigan is not just one place, but many. There's the Michigan of auto plants and furniture factories, of iron and copper mines, of soybeans and sugar beets and Christmas tree plantations. There's the Michigan of the Great Lakes—of pristine sand beaches and spectacular rocky shorelines and some of the best freshwater fishing in the world. There's the Michigan of universities and research centers and schools of the arts. Of clear-water lakes and tea-colored rivers. Of the Mackinac Bridge and Mackinac Island. Of jack pine barrens and coastal wetlands and remnant prairies. Of forests where bear, moose, elk, deer, and wolf far outnumber humans. And there's a world of history to investigate: of Native American hunters, Great Lakes explorers, French fur-traders, a timber industry that made more profit in the nineteenth century than the California gold rush, of industrial innovations that changed the world. As with any place, the closer you look, the more there is to see.

Artists and writers delight in such variety. It's only fitting, then, that this book is the work of many artists instead of one. To see the many Michigans requires many pairs of eyes, many sensibilities, many perspectives. Taken together, they add up to a portrait that captures a sense of the place as well as any book I know.

But of course it's not the real Michigan. You can see that only for yourself. Best to go on foot or in a canoe. If you must go by car, take backroads and two-tracks, and drive slowly, with the windows down, so you can smell sweet fern and wild rose. Chat with locals at country stores and cafes. Get chewed on by mosquitoes. Get caught in a snowstorm. Get some sand in your shoes.

Most importantly, take your time. The true character of the place will come to you, but don't expect it to happen overnight. It's a big state, after all, with many secret rooms. Think of it as a vacation that lasts a lifetime.

PREFACE

As a publisher of Great Lakes regional titles, we at Thunder Bay Press take great pride in our books and our home state of Michigan. Views of Michigan was originally conceived in a conversation among our chief editors. The idea: to publish a new and creative photography book which would capture the many unique "views" of the vast state of Michigan.

Rather than contracting select photographers or searching for individual photographs, Thunder Bay Press held a photography contest. The contest was advertised at Michigan colleges, through regional photography clubs, as well as on the Thunder Bay Press website and Facebook page.

After a few months of advertising, the photographs began to arrive. They were varied and intriguing, taken by resident photographers of all levels of experience. Having received many submissions, it wasn't easy to select the winners. We spent days around a conference table strewn with photographs, attempting to single out images which best expressed the essence of Michigan.

The process resulted in the pages that follow, an exploration of the renown and hidden places of Michigan. Scattered with scenes from across the region, each turn of the page reveals the majesty of the state. These "views" have been captured by a group of incredibly skillful Michigan photographers, and we hope you enjoy every one.

The Editors of
Thunder Bay Press

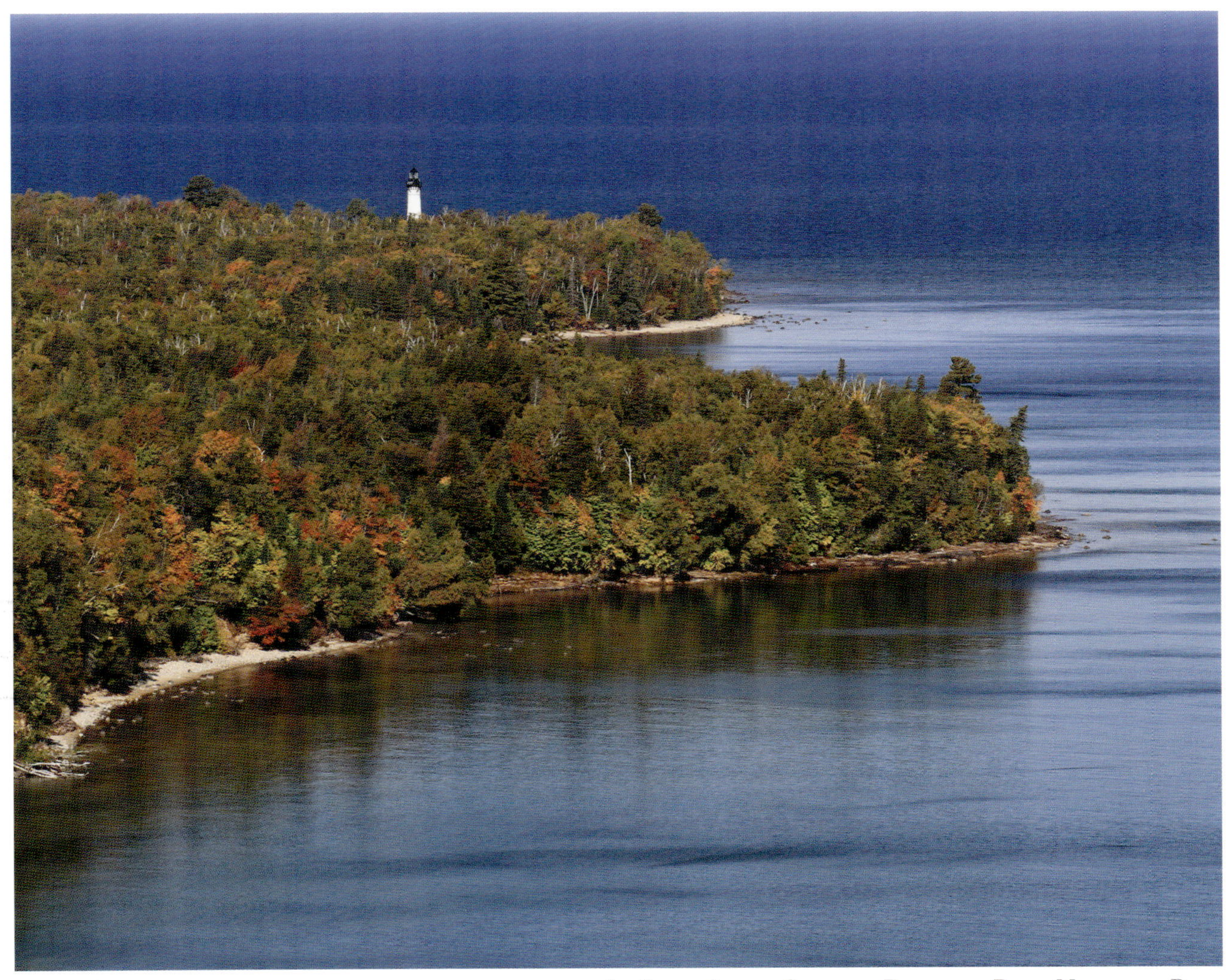

Julien Brasseur

Au Sable Light Station, Pictured Rock National Park

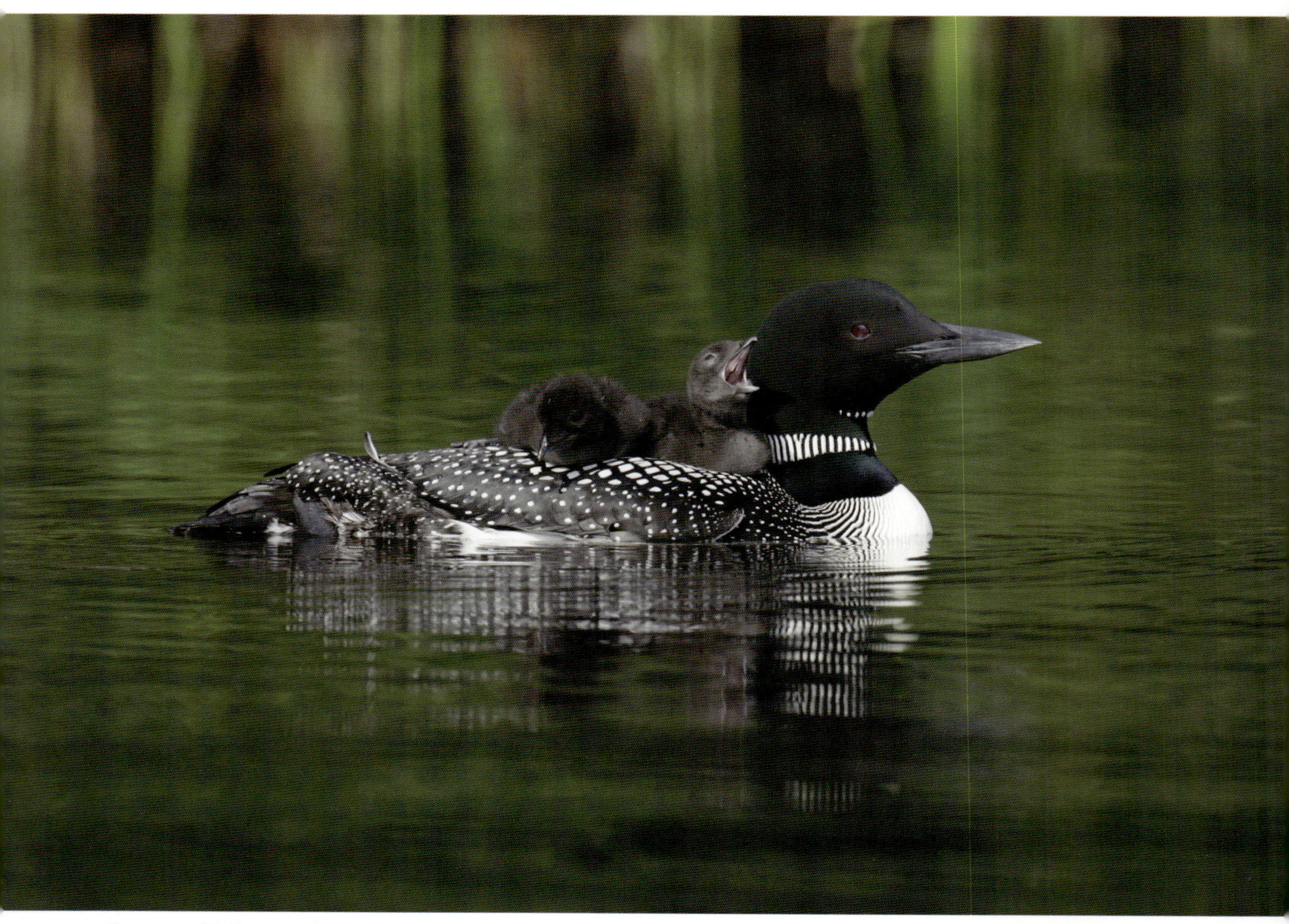

Stephen R. Sage

Common Loon with Chicks, Presque Isle

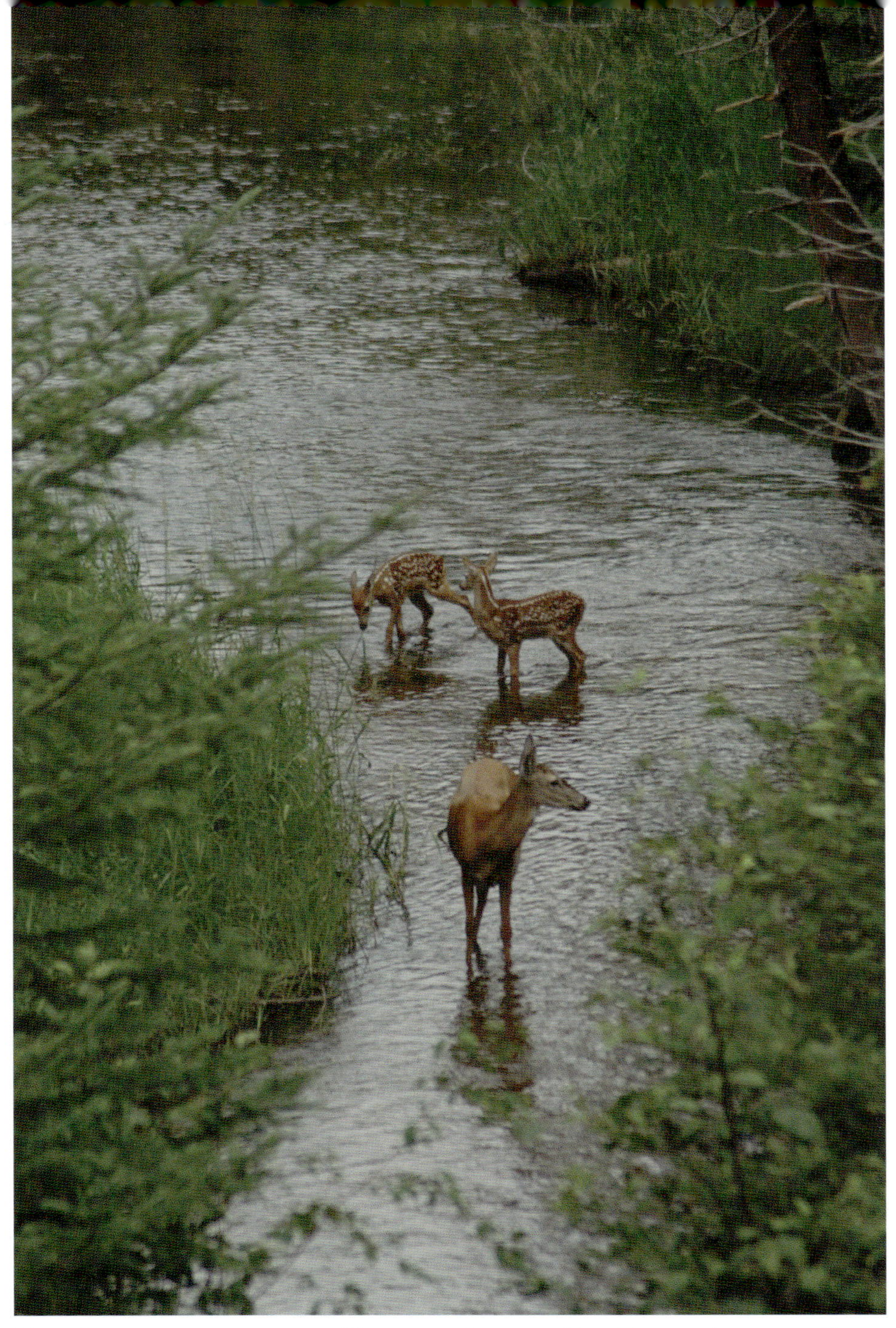

Dove Day　　Whitetail Doe and Two Fawns, Sturgeon River

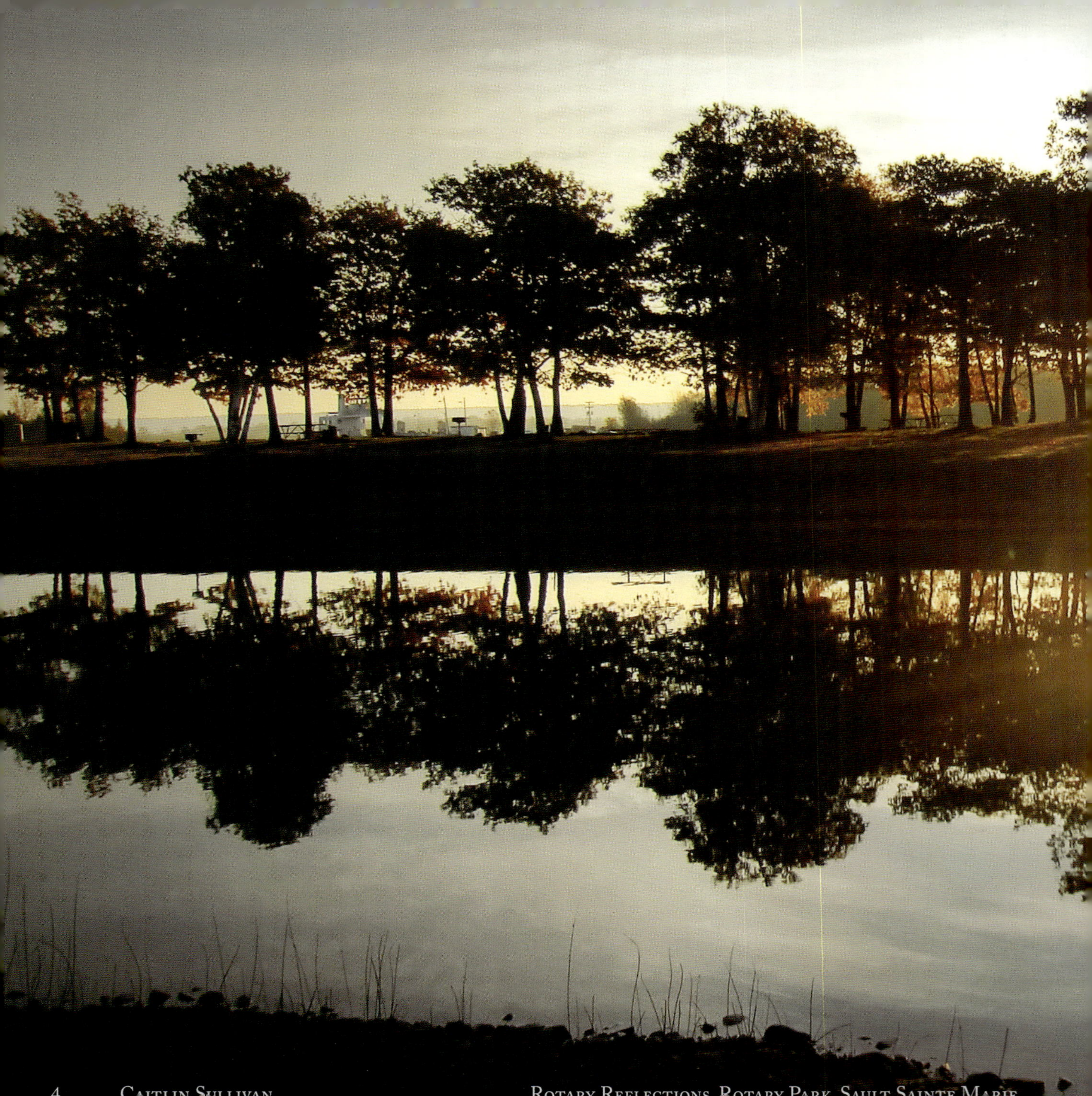

Caitlin Sullivan

Rotary Reflections, Rotary Park, Sault Sainte Marie

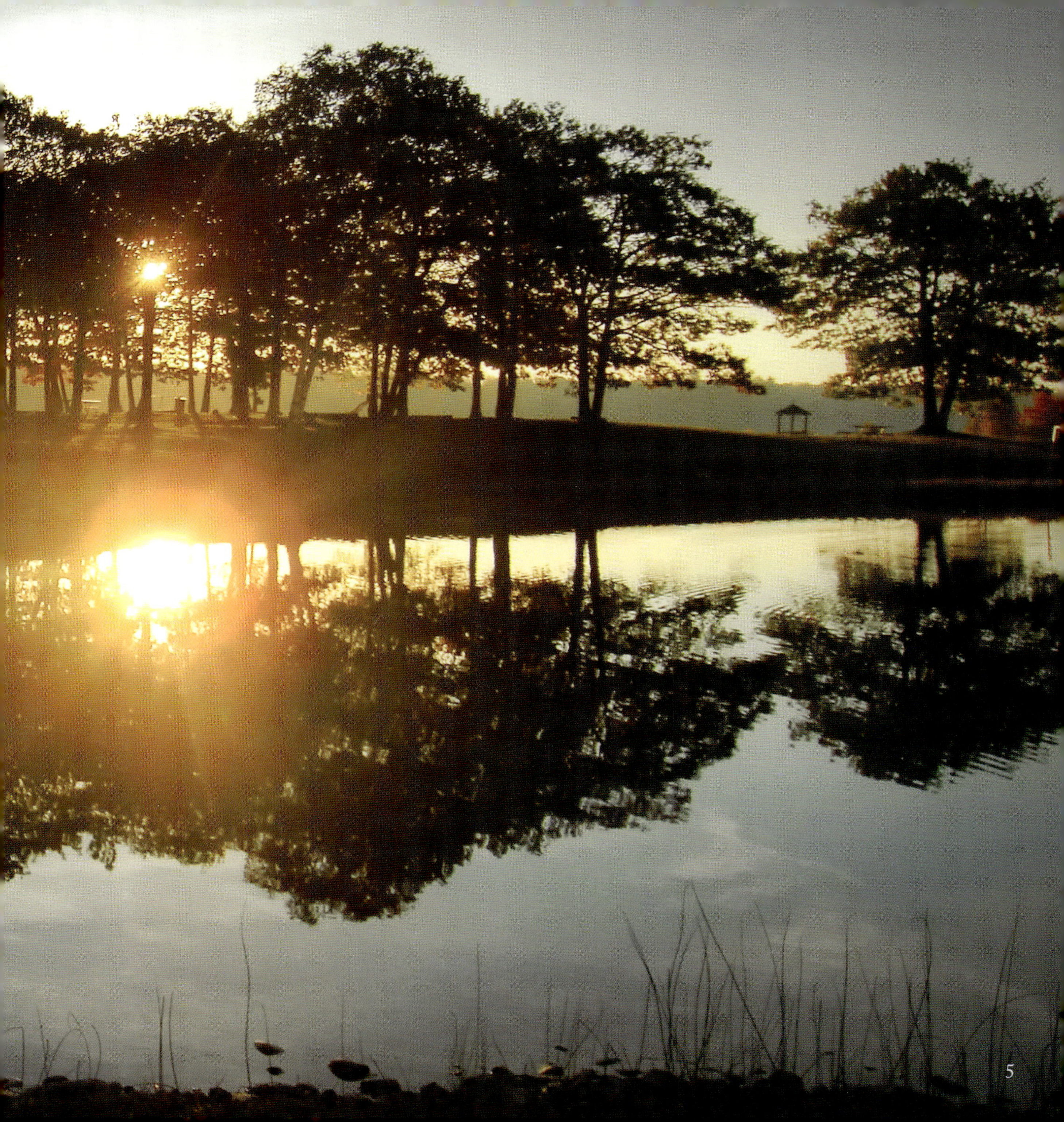

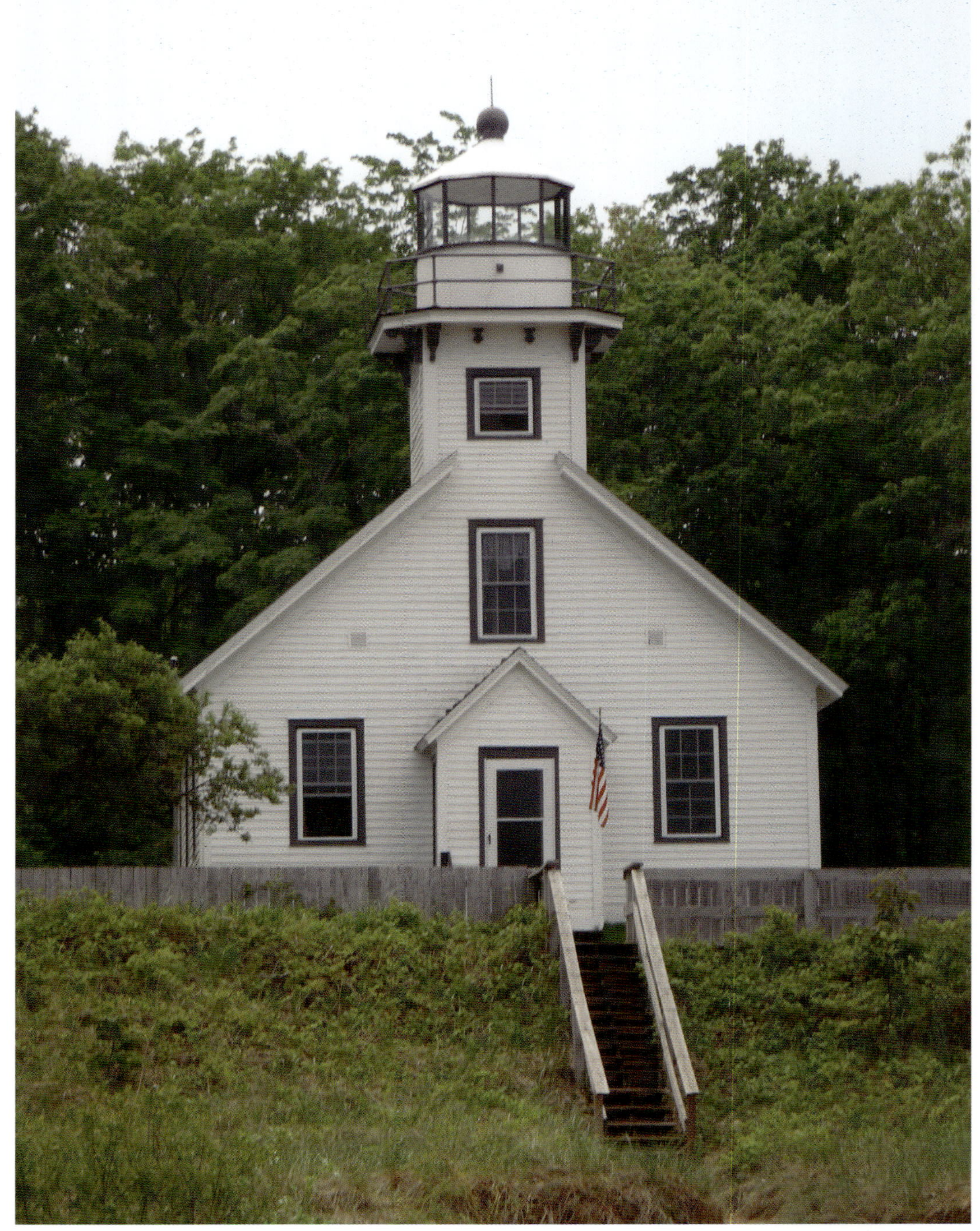

Julie Taylor

Old Mission Point Lighthouse, Grand Traverse

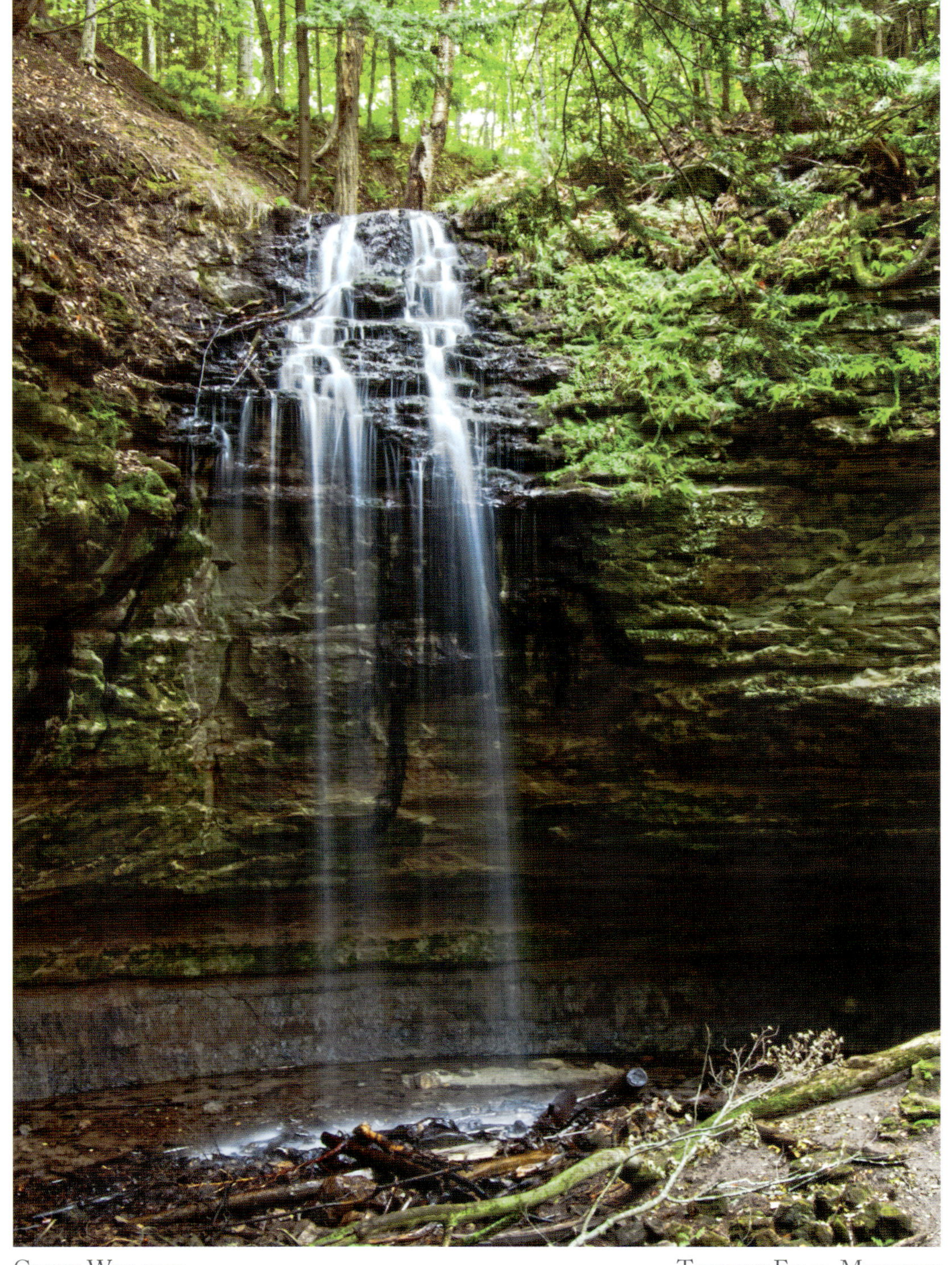

Cyndy Williams

Tannery Falls, Munising

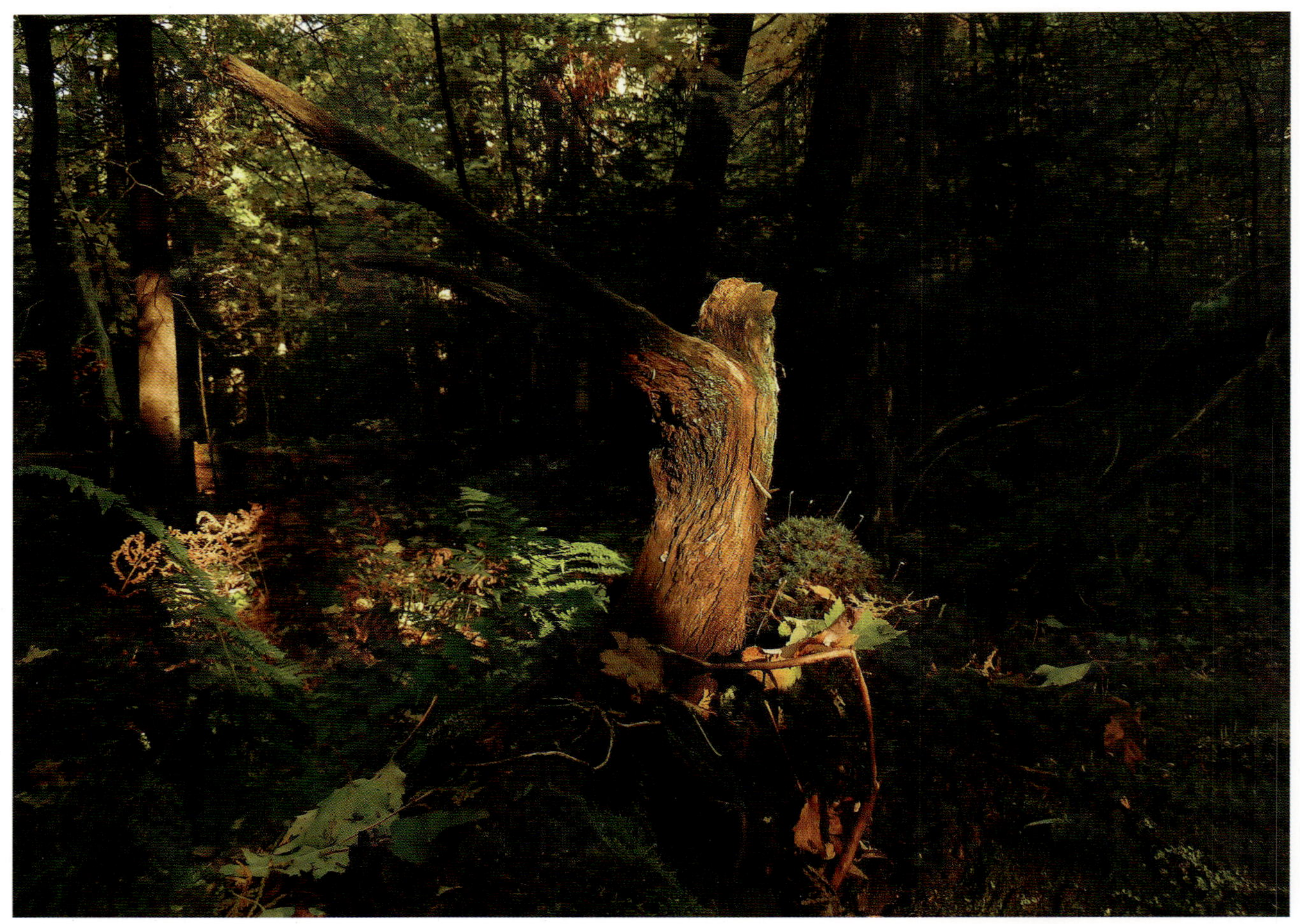

Mike Irolla — Reaching For the Light, Chocolay Township

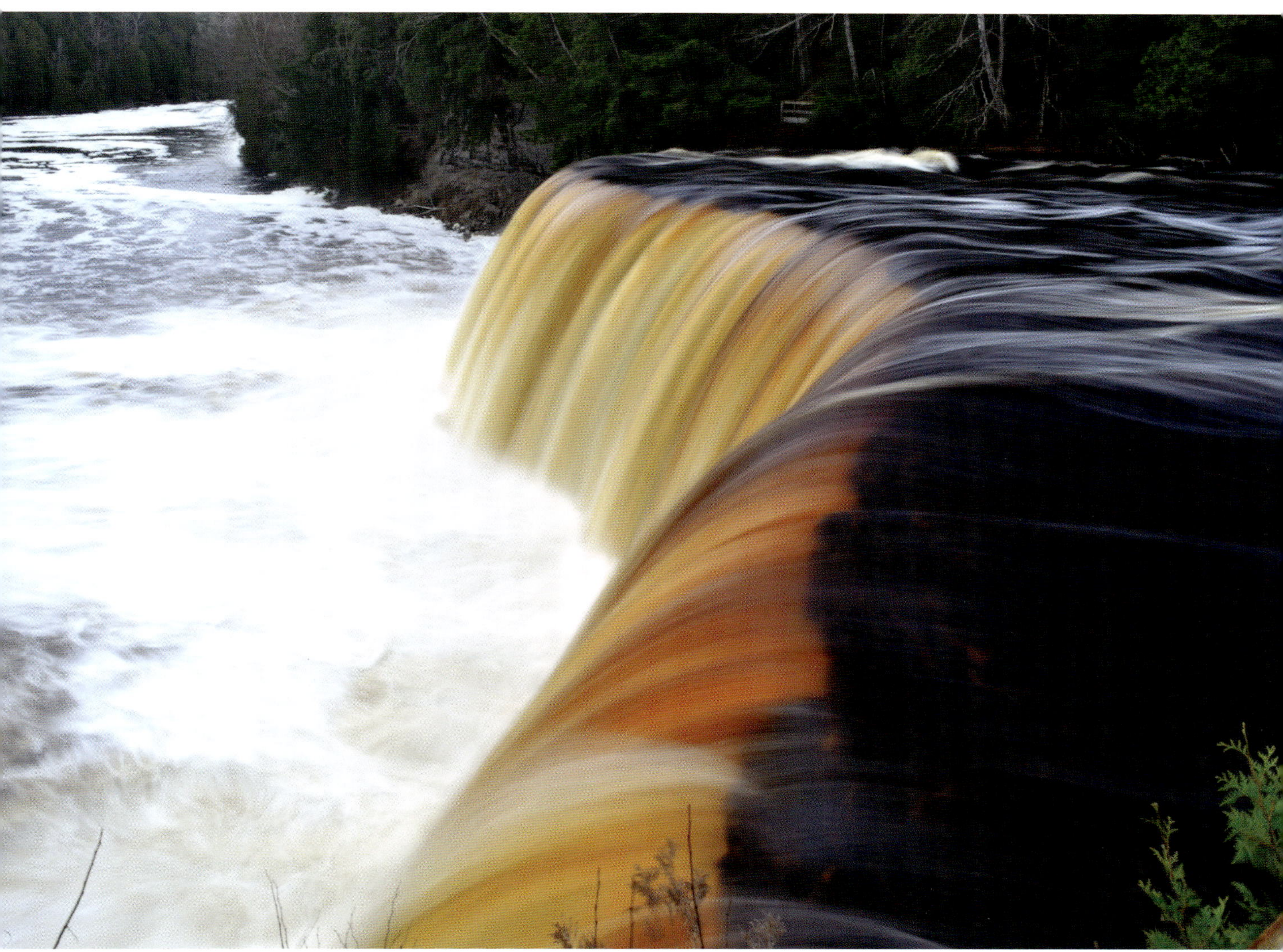

Courtney Cochran

Upper Falls, Tahquamenon Falls State Park

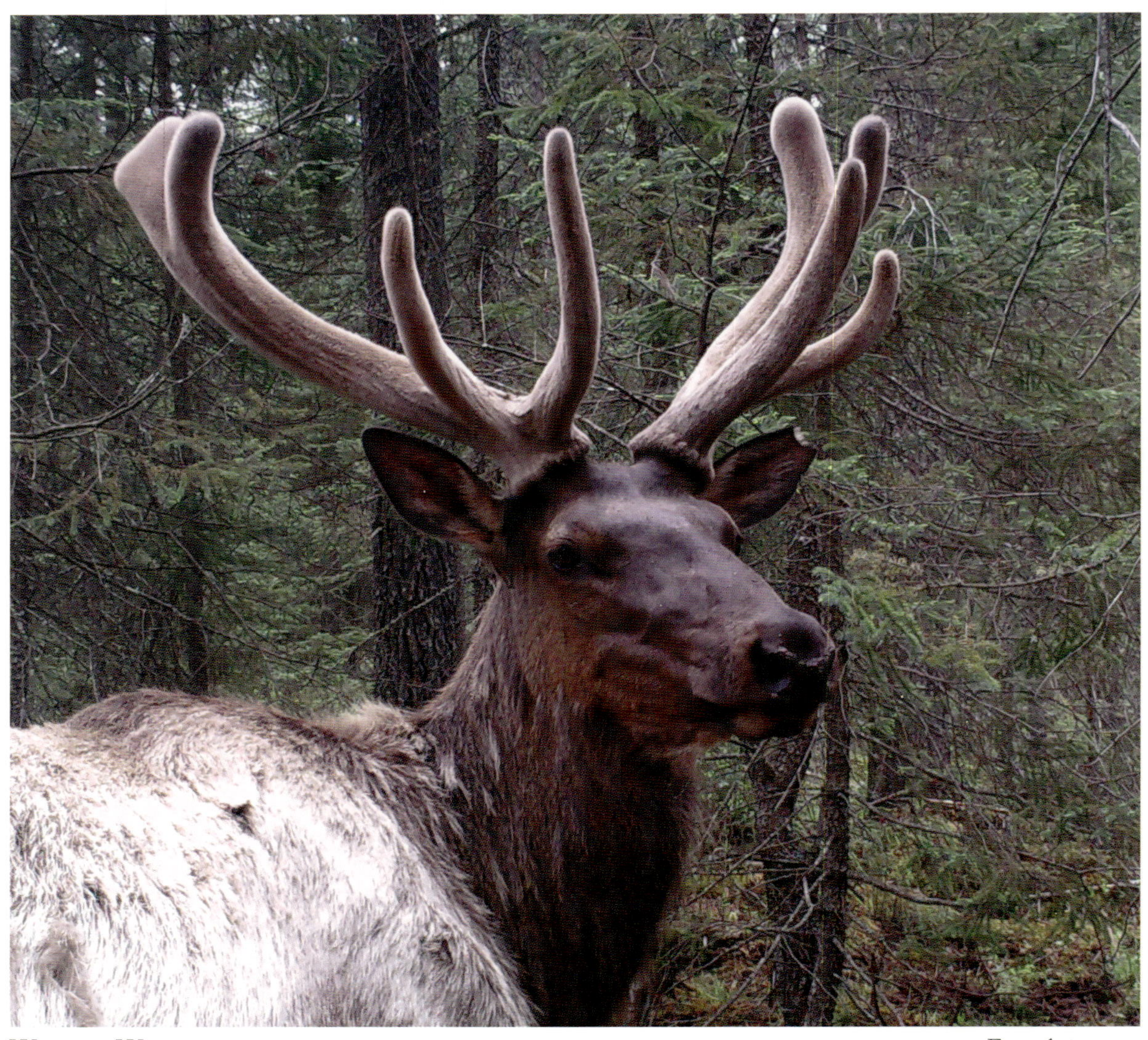

Webster Wood — Elk, Atlanta

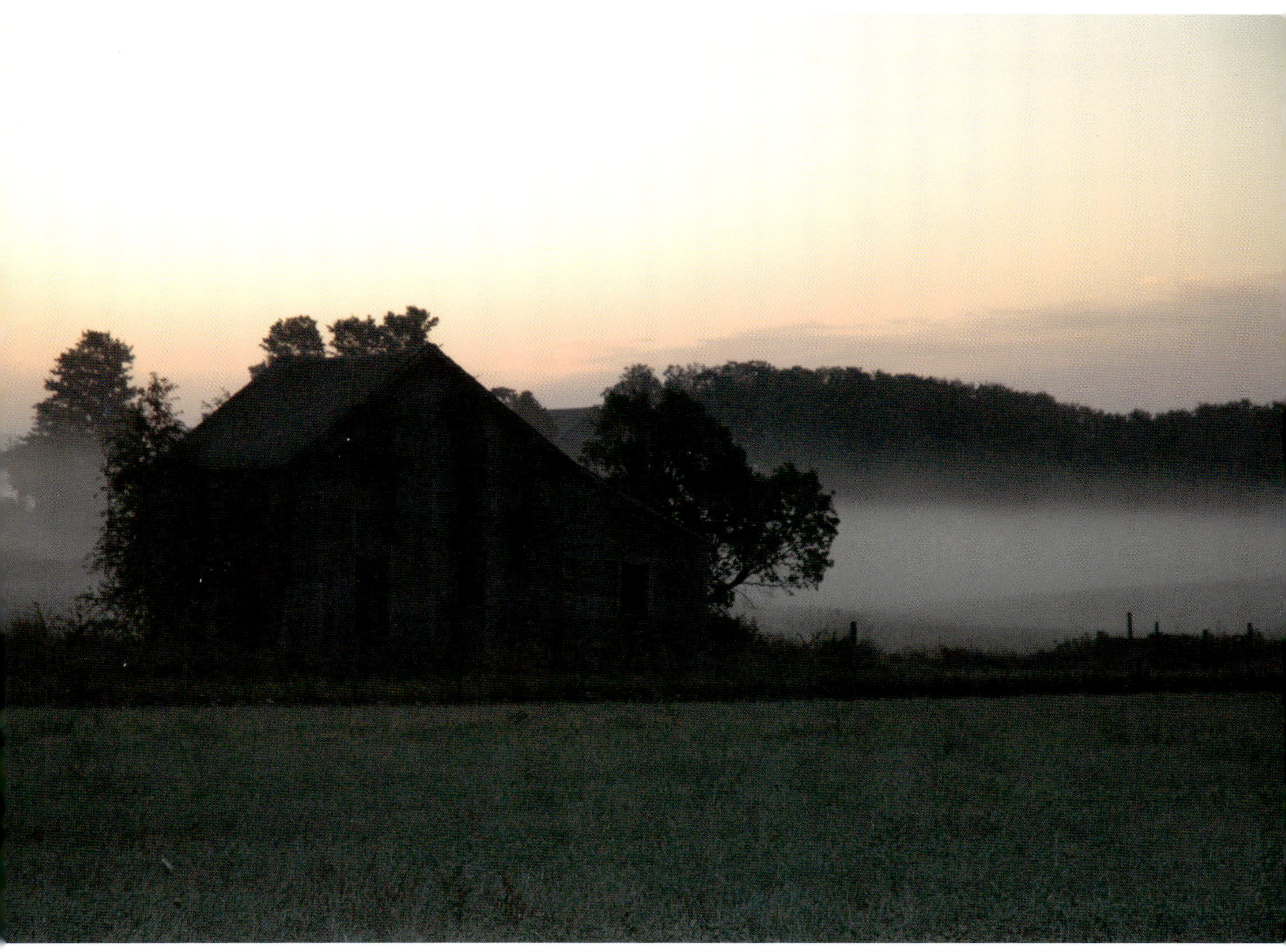

Dove Day — Old Abandoned Farm House in Early Morning Fog, Petoskey

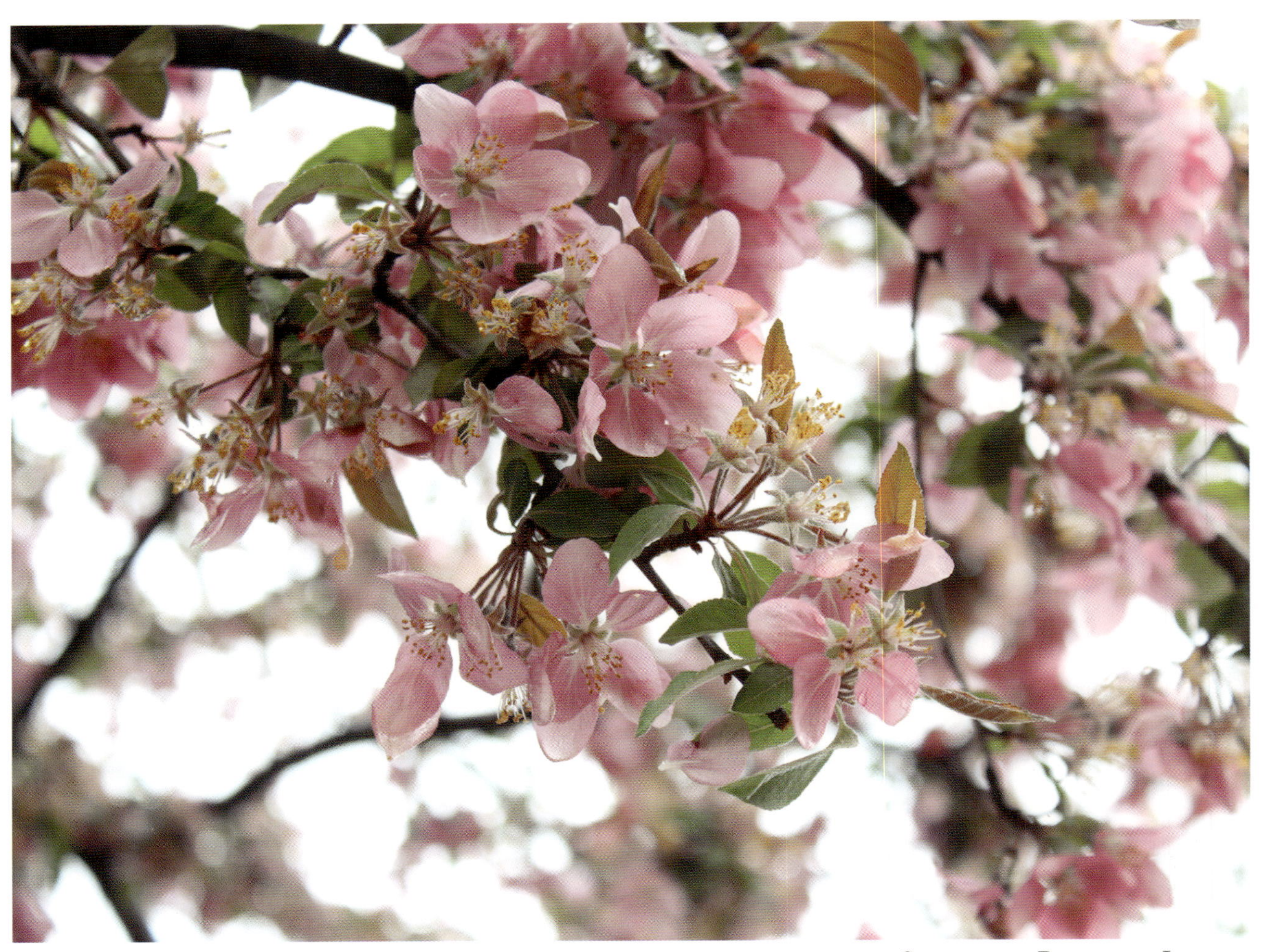

Jacquelyn Dawson

Springtime Blossoms, Jackson

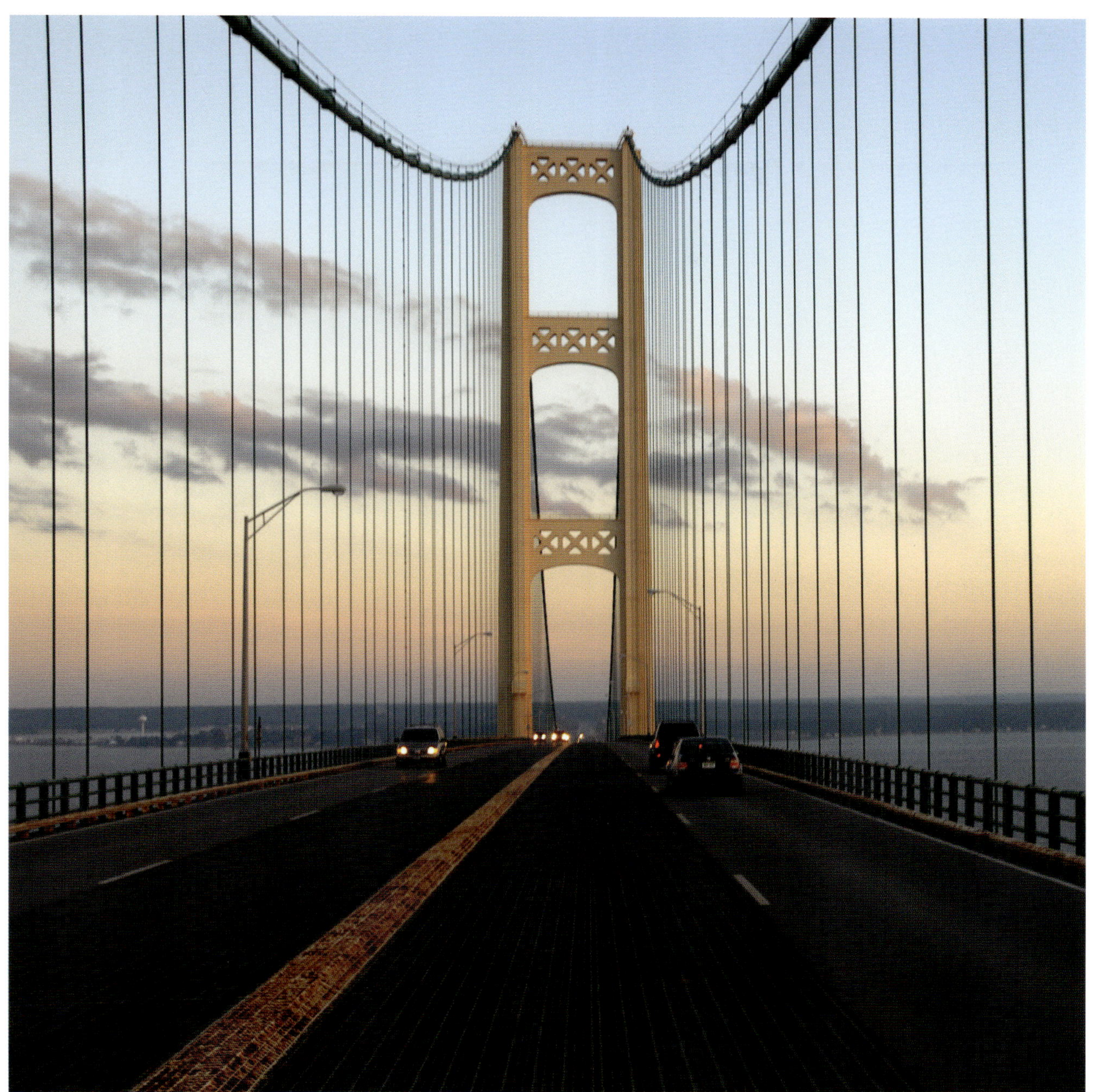

Loren S. Shattuck

Mackinac Bridge, Mackinaw City – St. Ignace

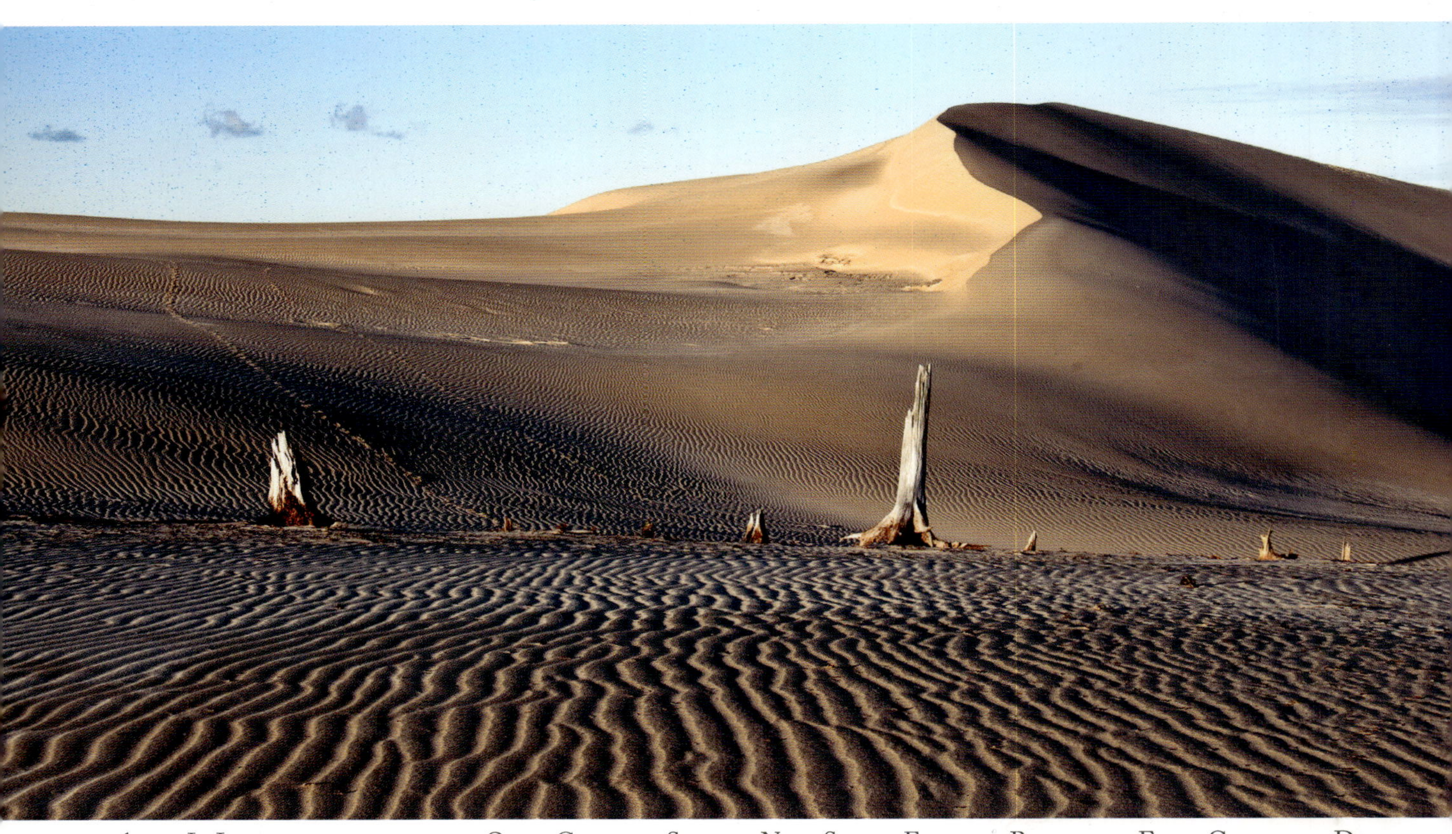

Alan L. Jones

Once Covered Stumps Now Stand Exposed Before an Ever-Changing Dune, Silver Lake State Park

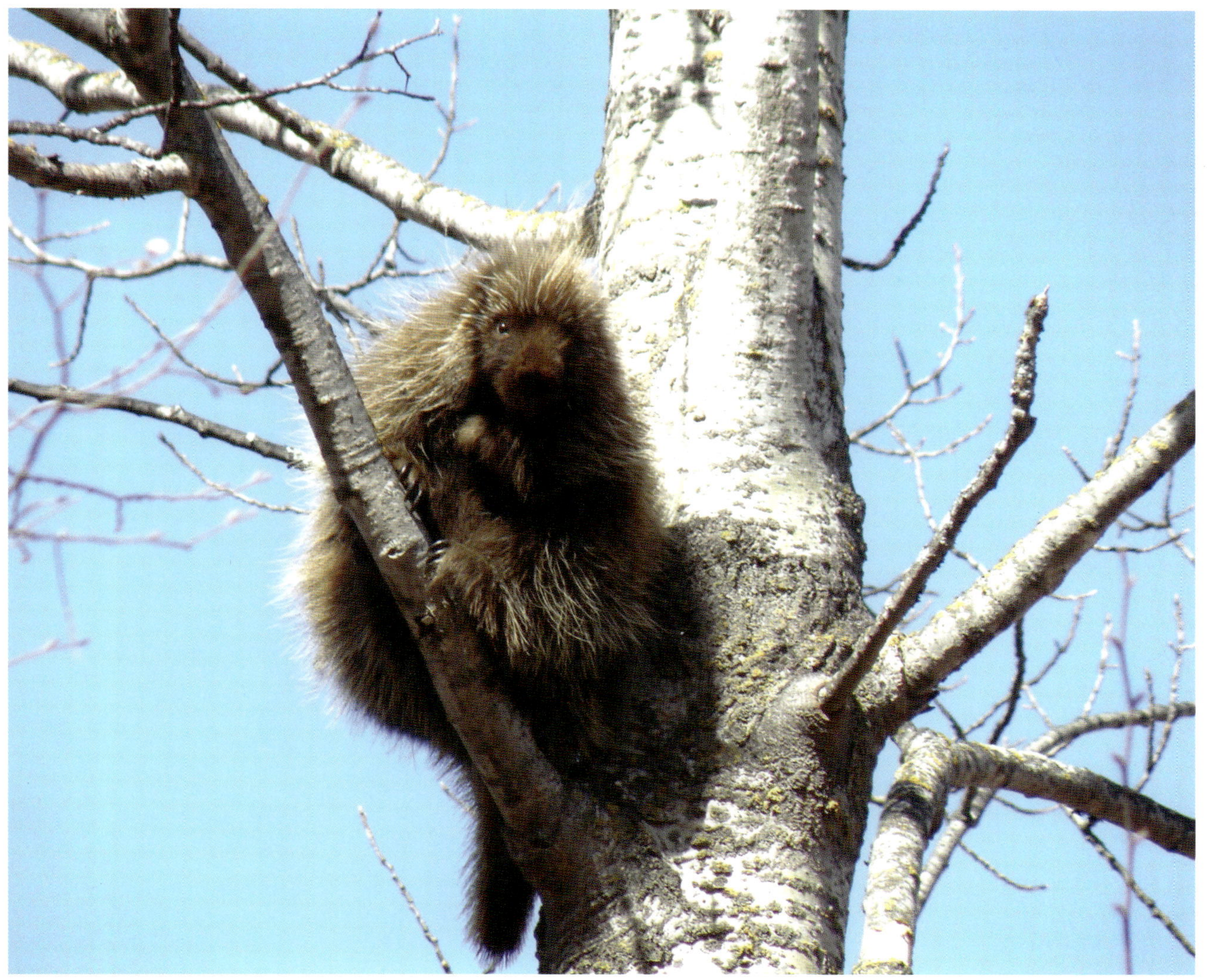

Marion J. Wood

Porcupine, Atlanta

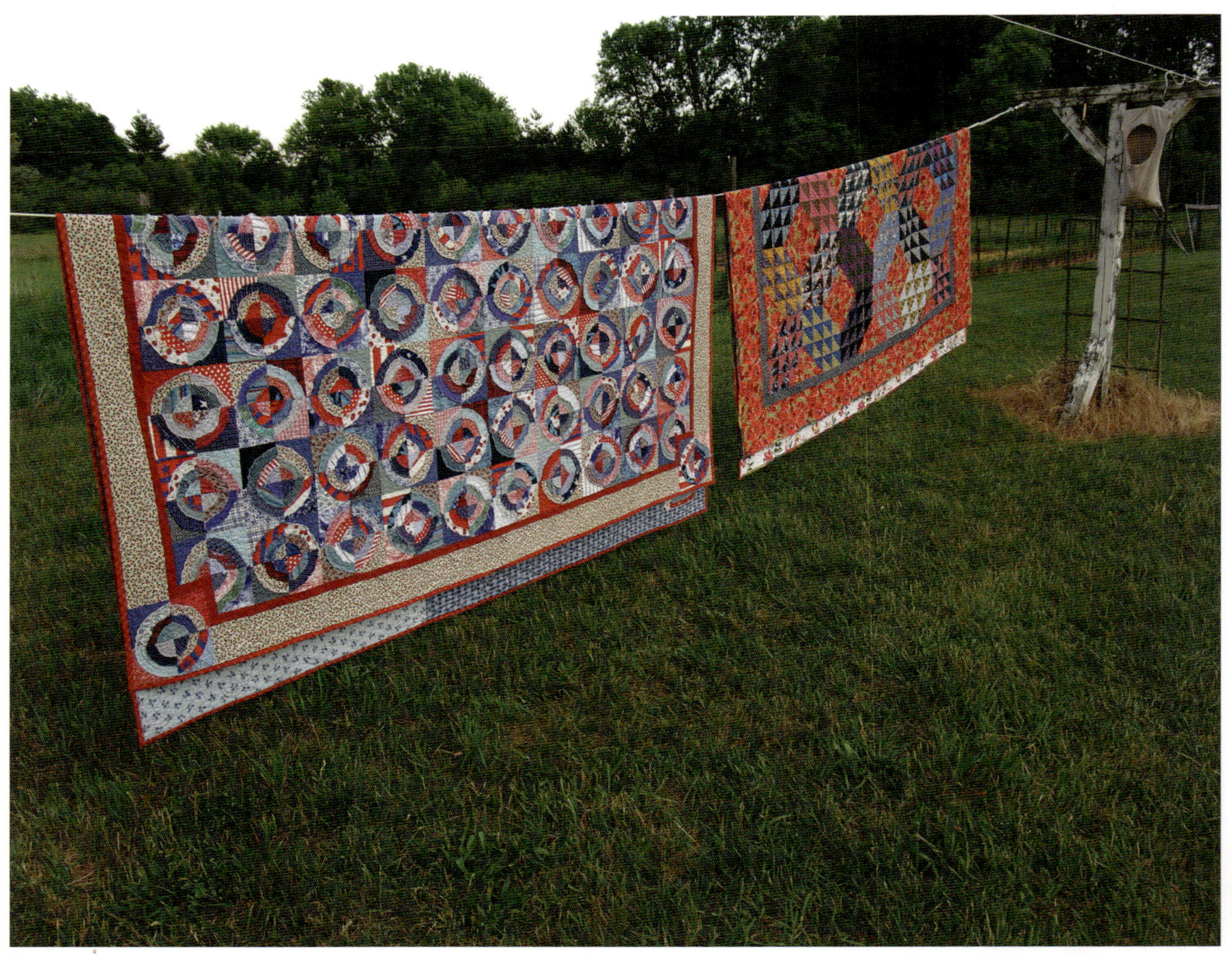

Rebecca Allen   Friend's Quilts, Laingsburg

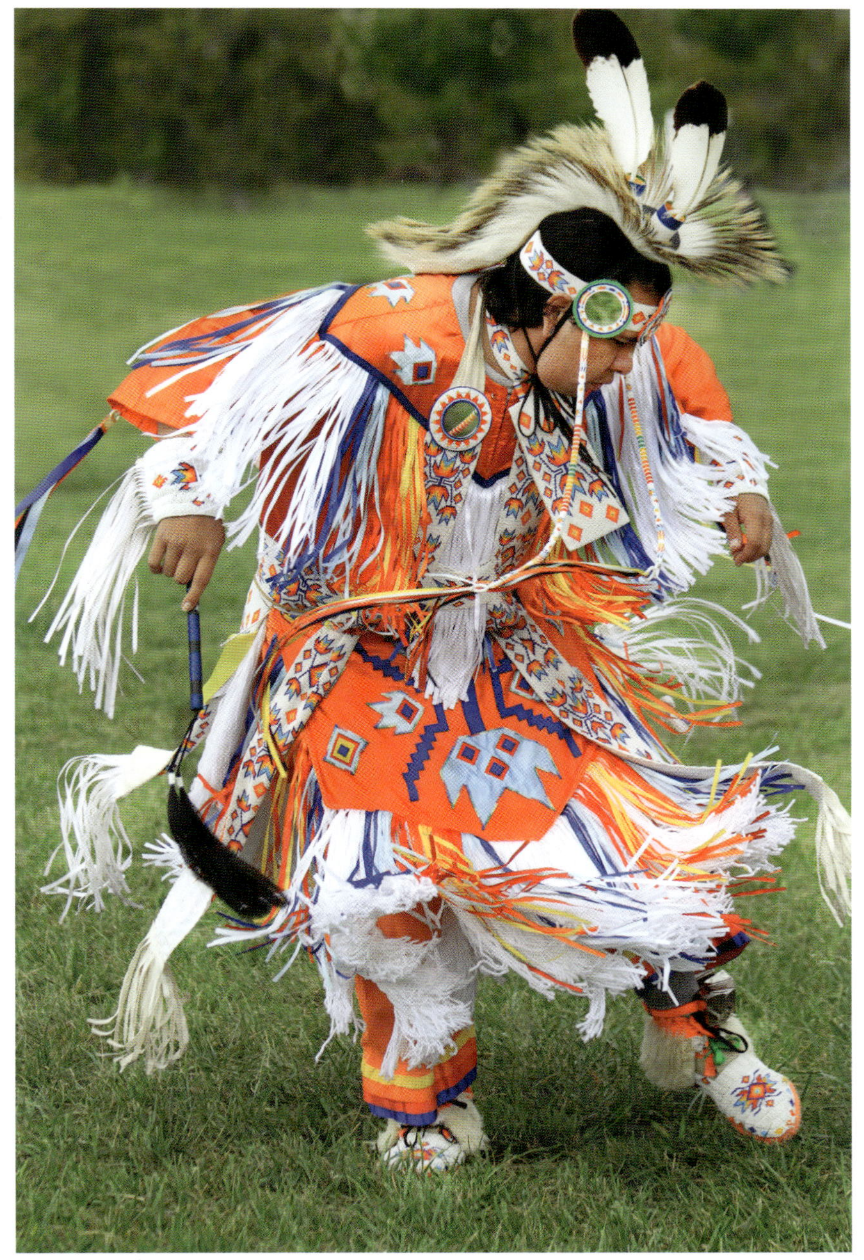

Brita Brookes Travis Schuyler dances at the American Indian Health and Family Services Pow Wow, Detroit

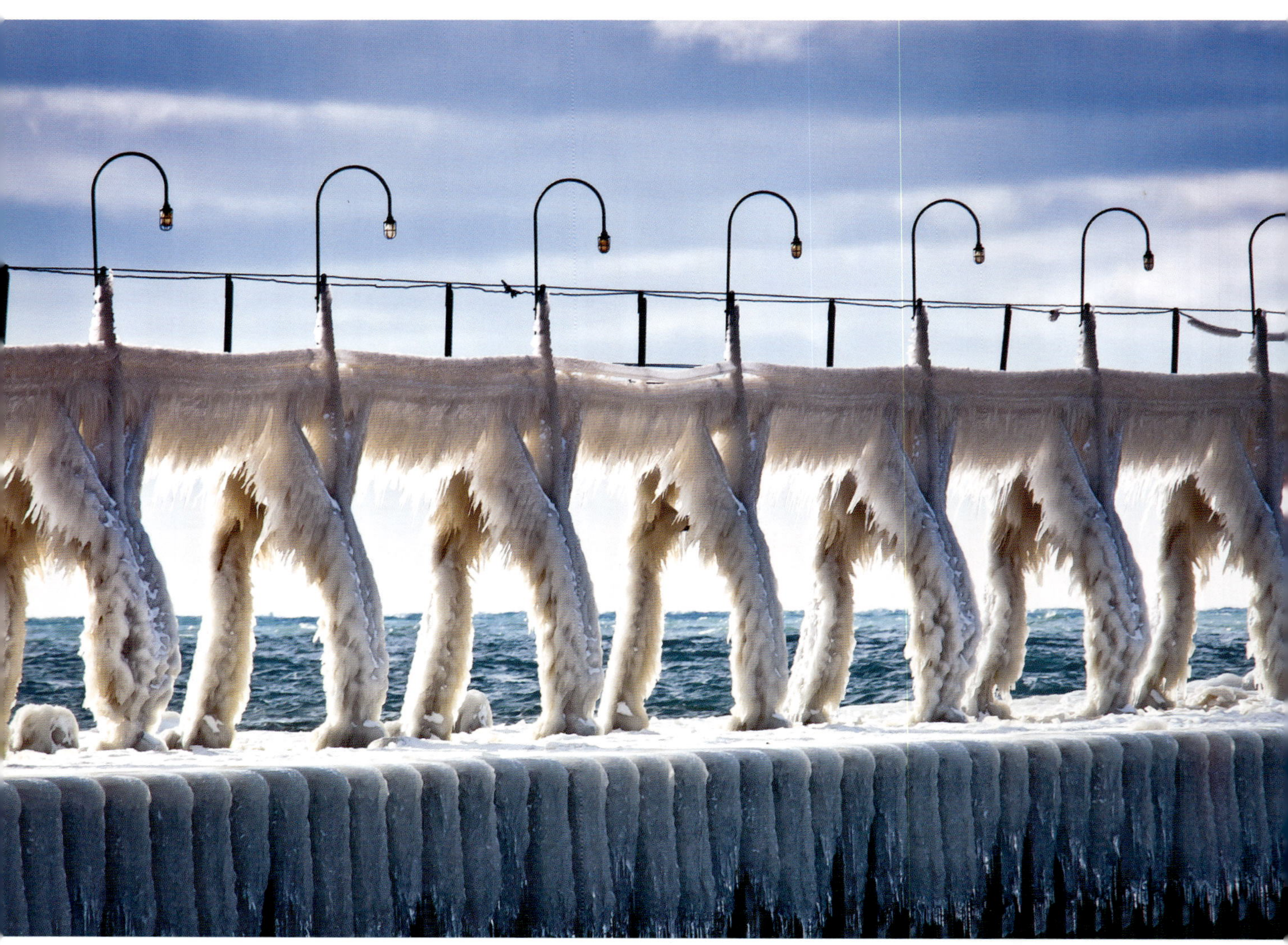

Dennis H. Guthrie

Walking Icemen, South Haven

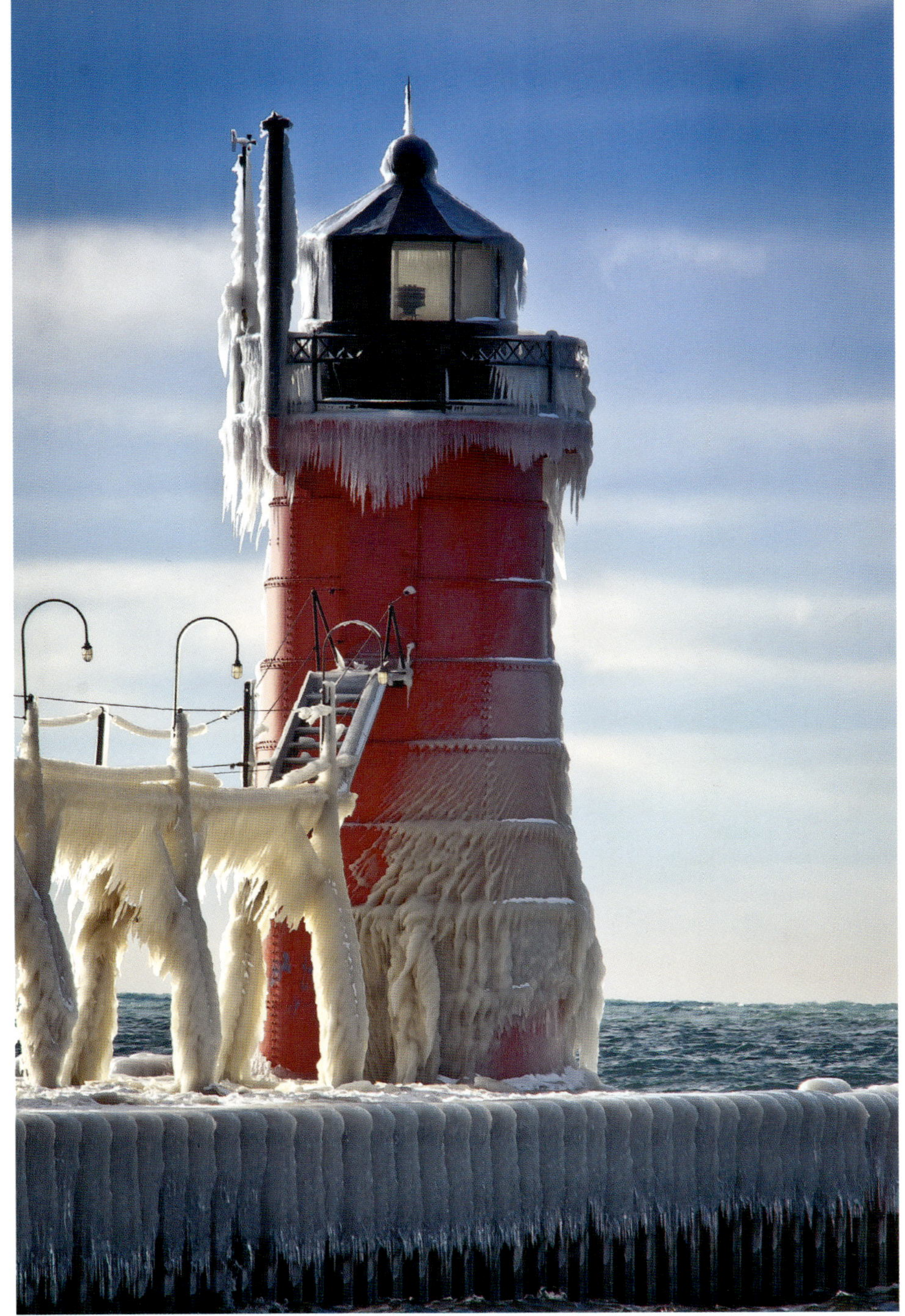

Dennis H. Guthrie Winter Candy Cane, South Haven Lighthouse

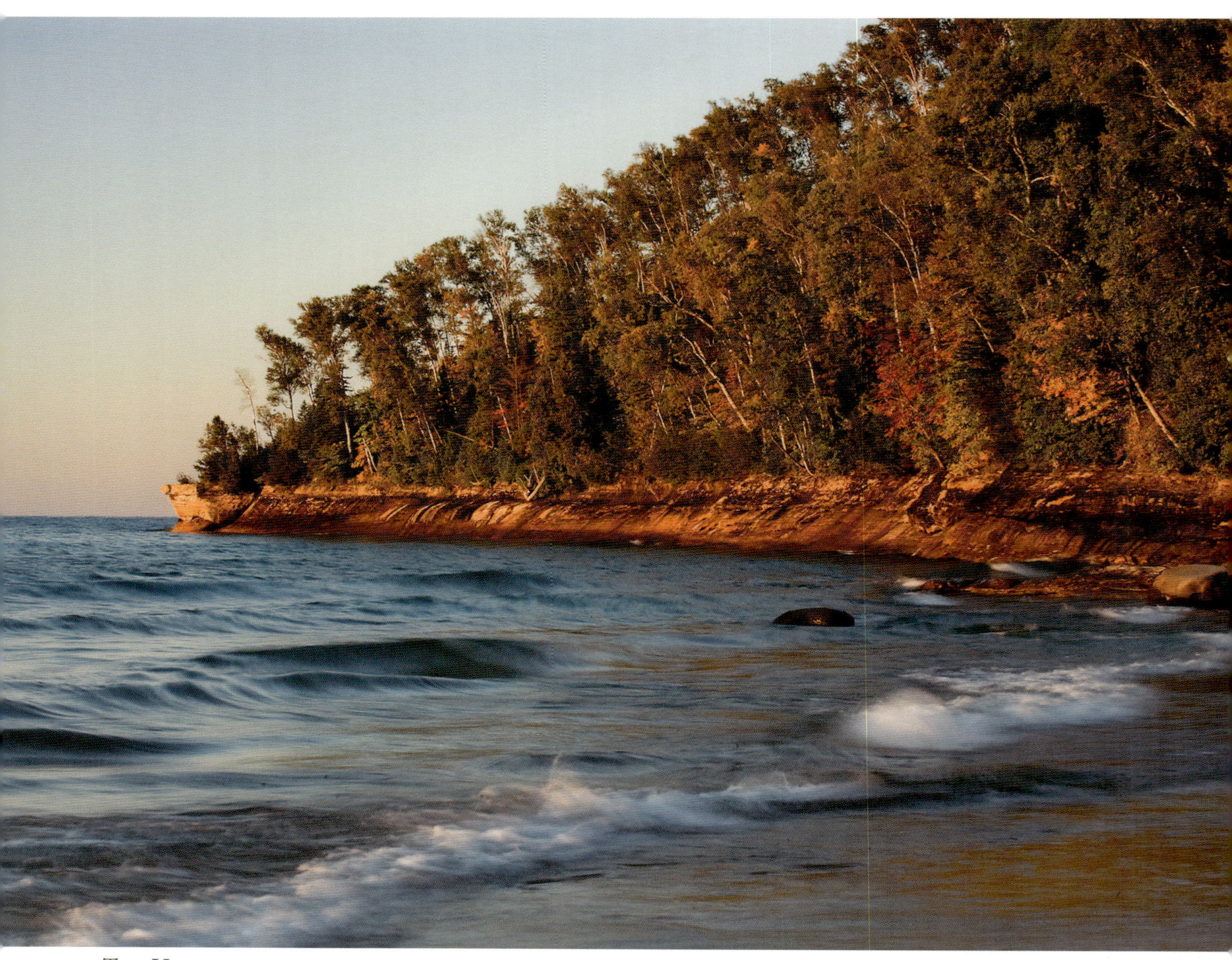

Tom Haxby

Lake Superior, Pictured Rocks National Lakeshore

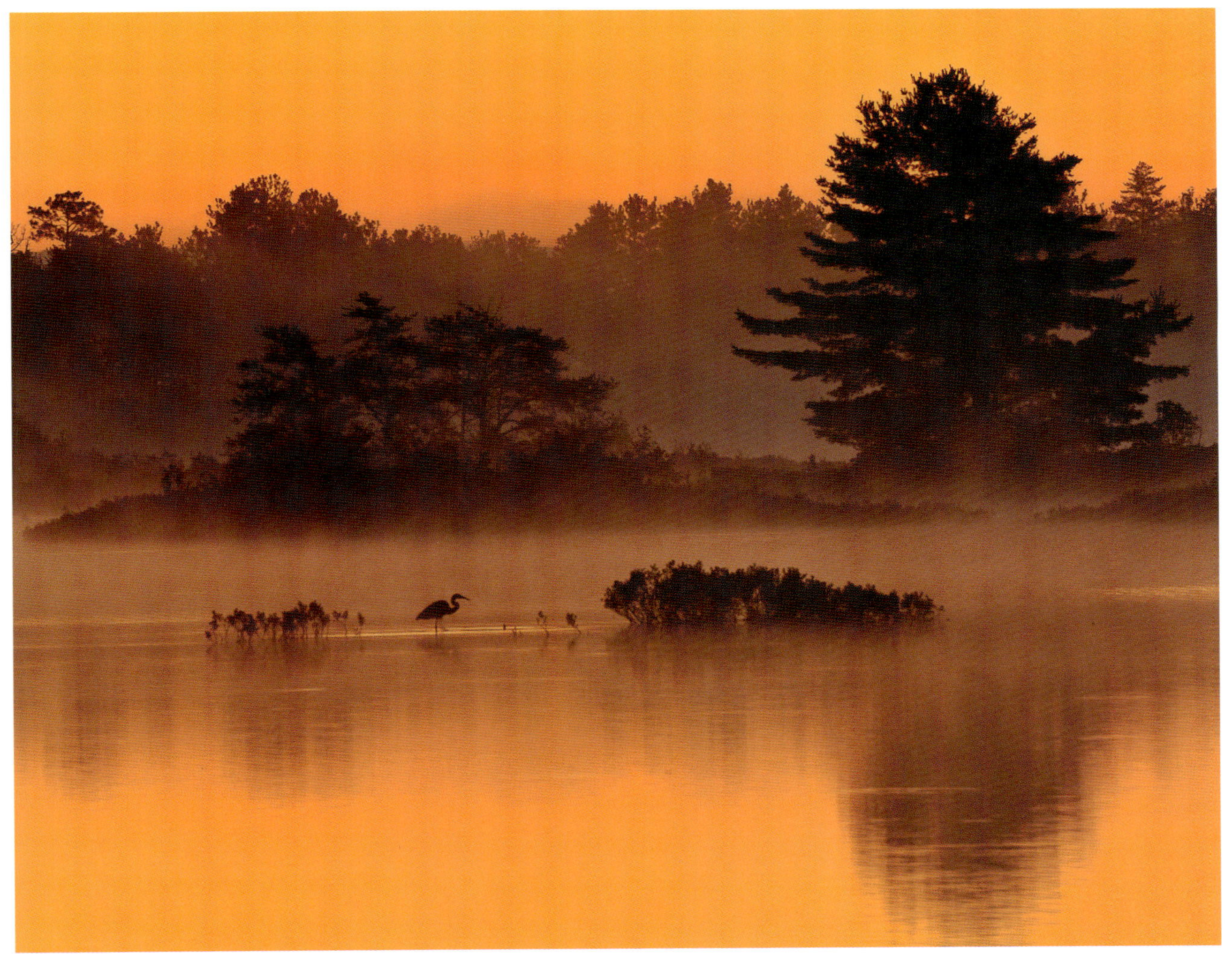

Alan L. Jones

Foggy Sunrise, Seney National Wildlife Refuge

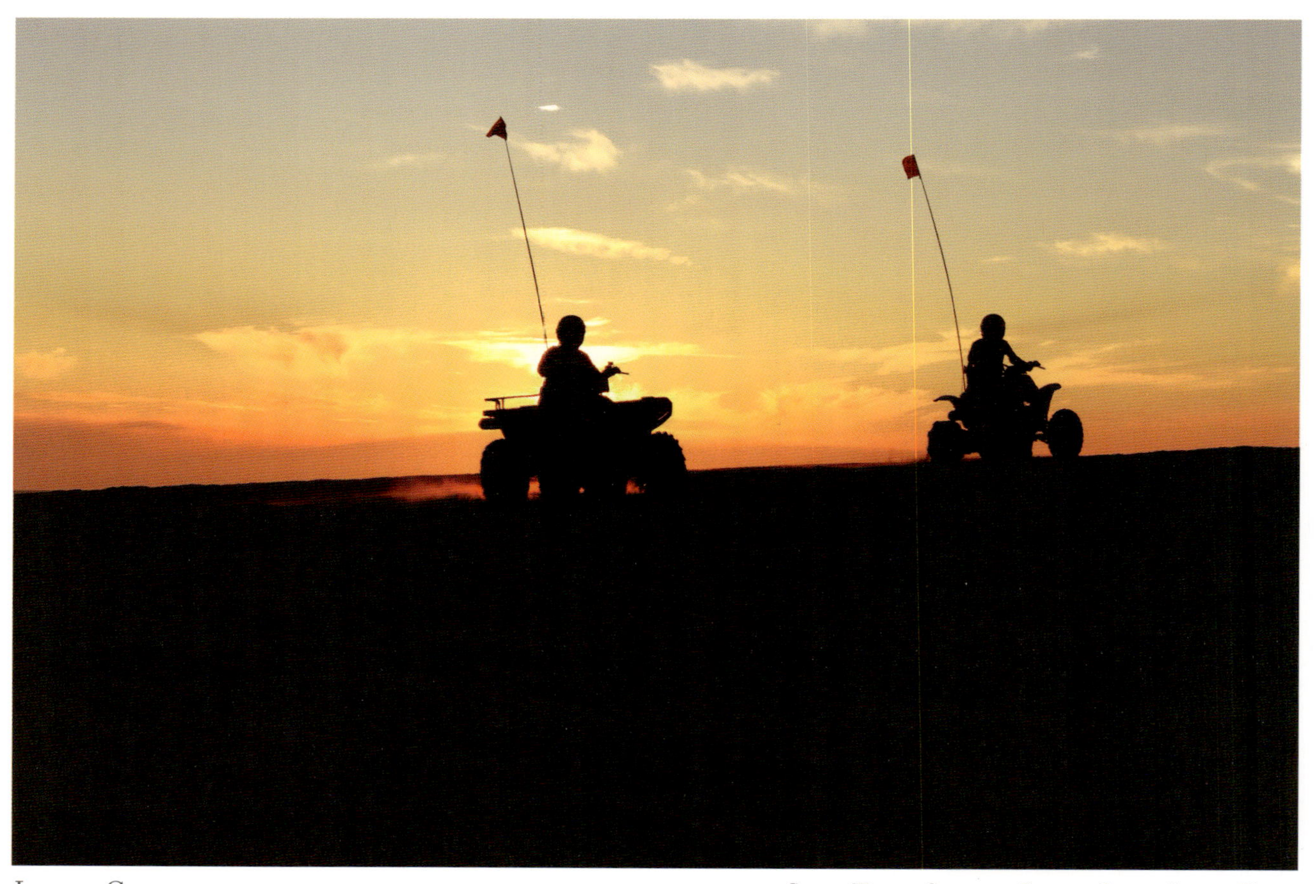

Ligang Chen

Sand Dune Sunset, Silver Lake State Park

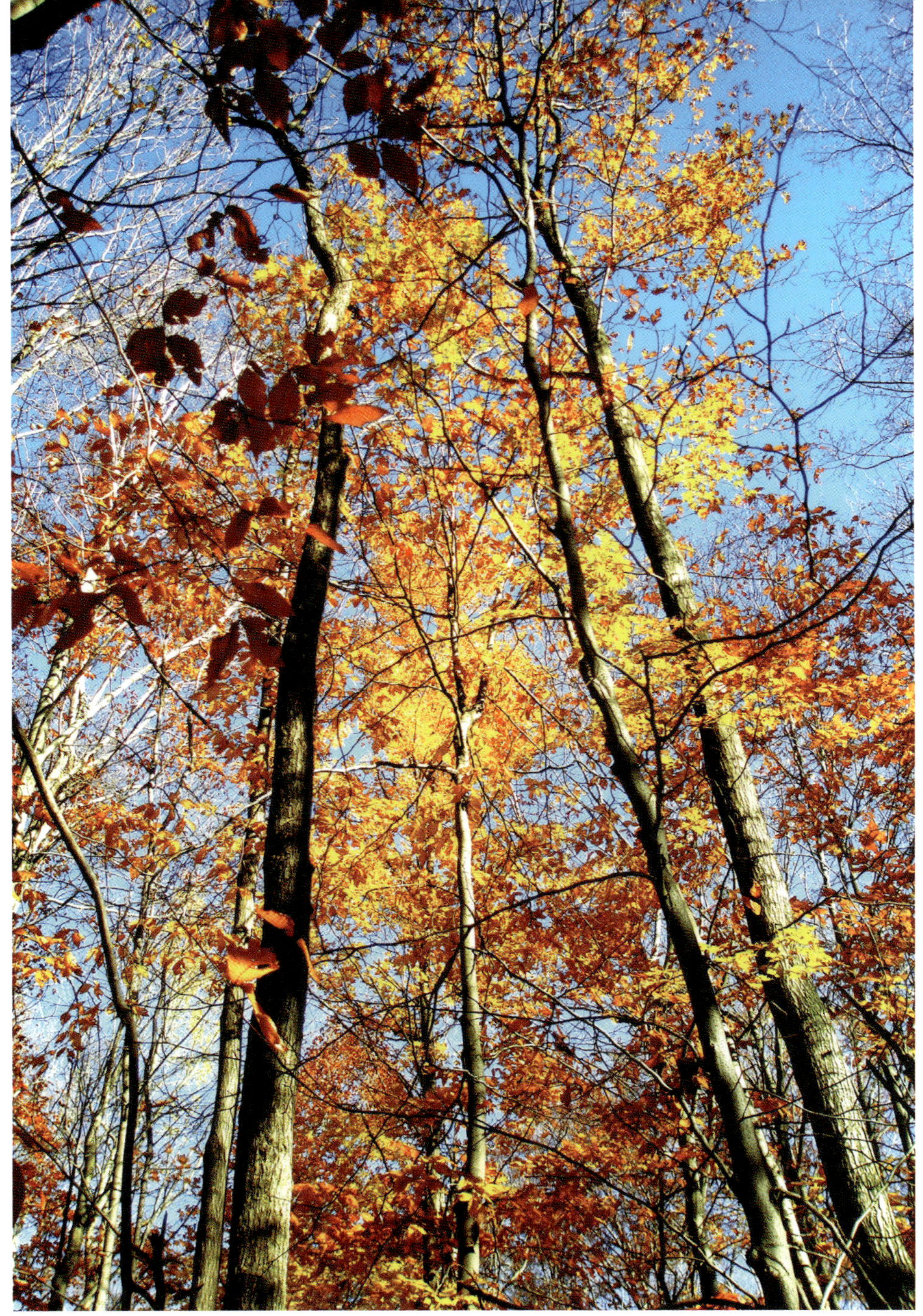

Jessi Bjorkman — Fall Color, Larks Lake, Pellston

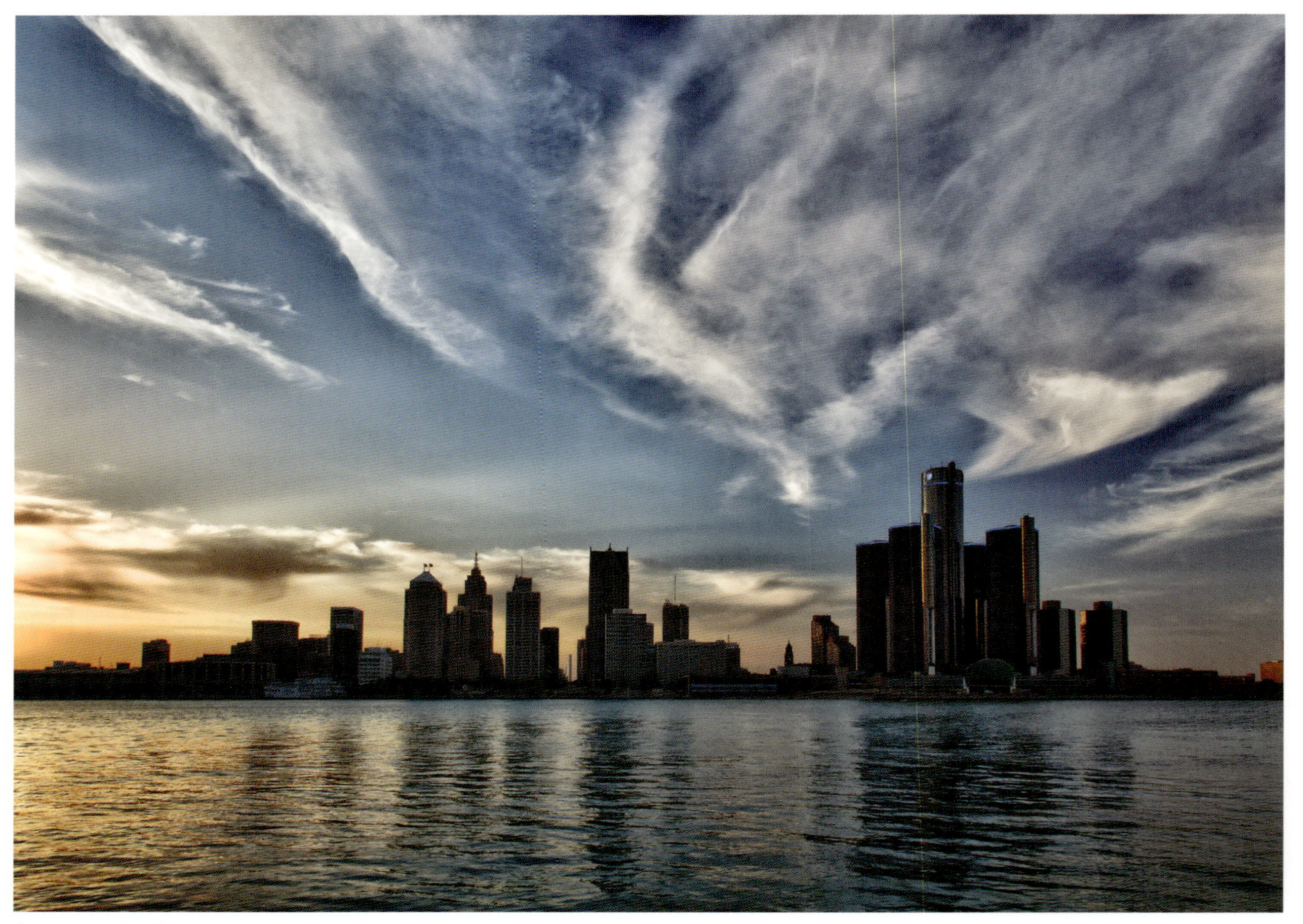

Stephen R. Sage

Detroit Skyline

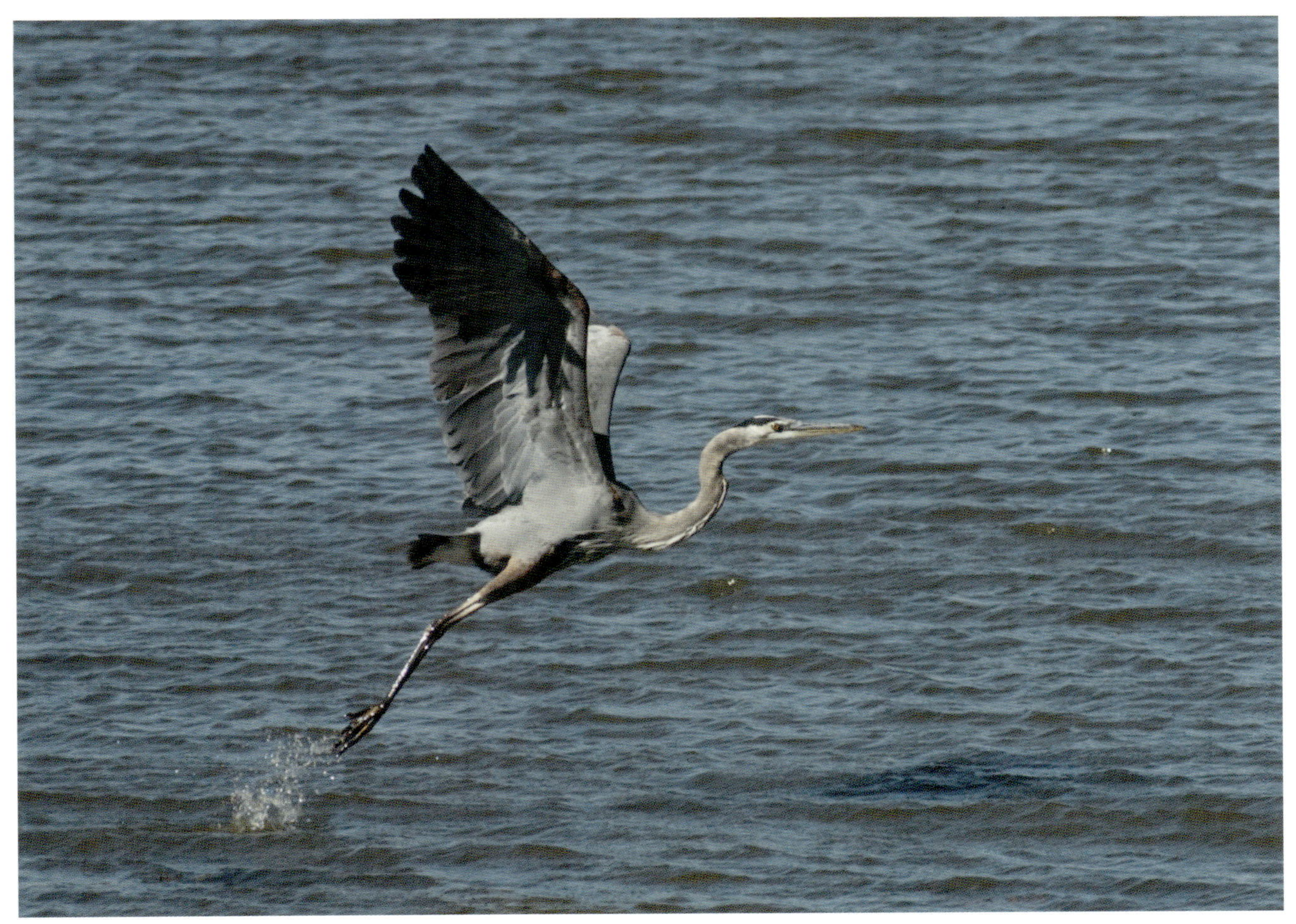

Cyndy Williams — Blue Heron Lift Off, Shiawassee National Wildlife Refuge

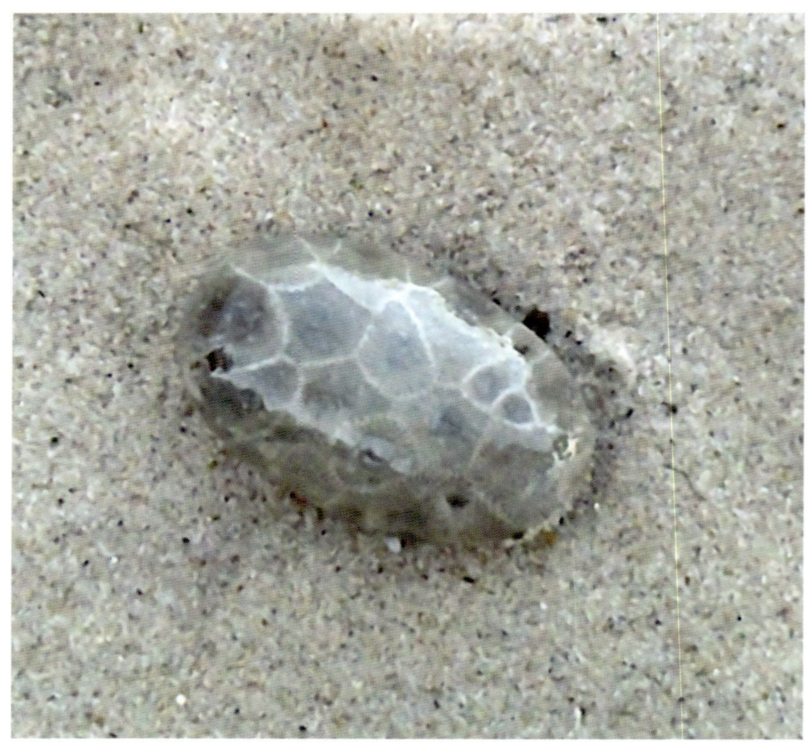

Mark Taylor Petoskey Stone, Fisherman's Island State Park

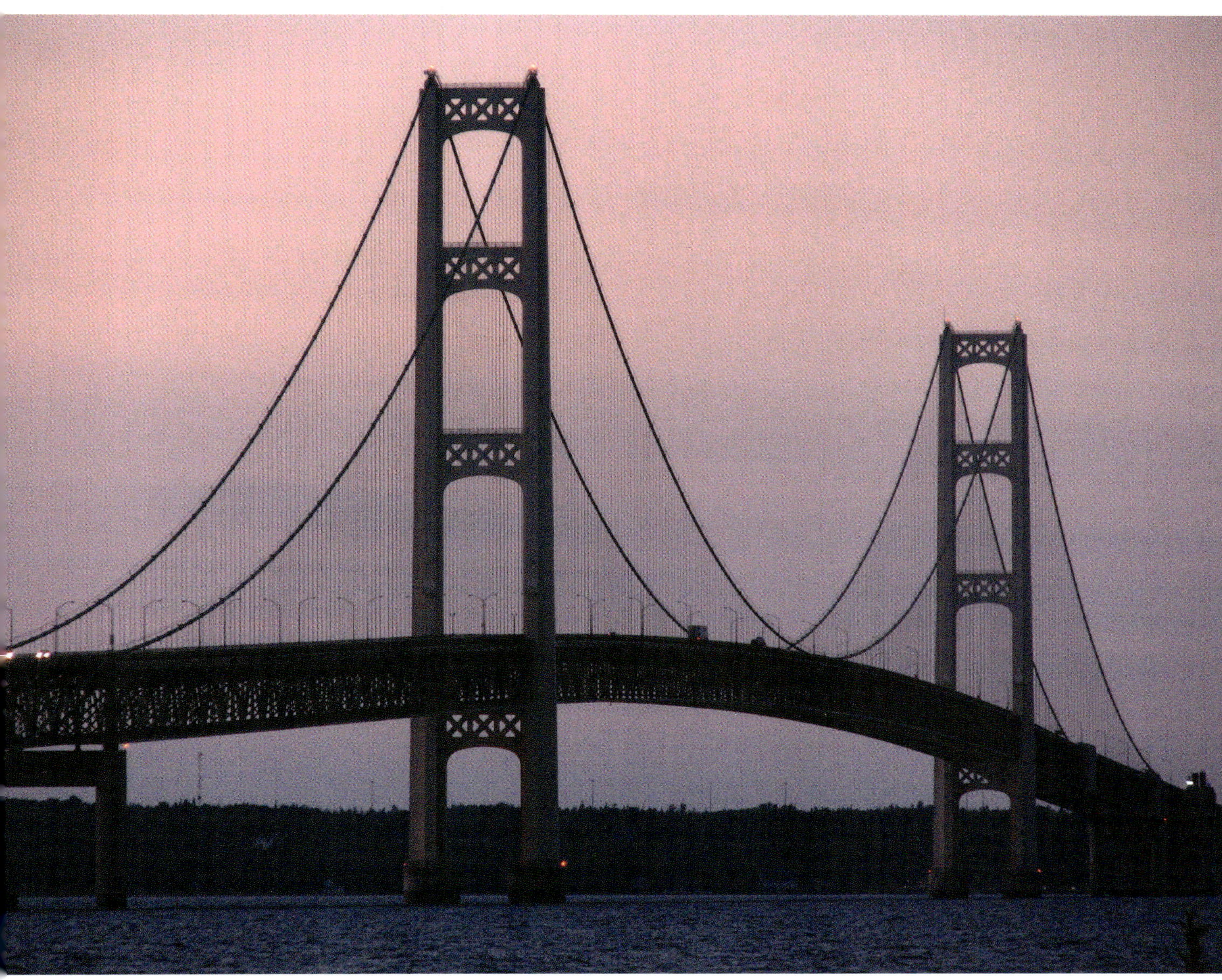

Loren S. Shattuck

Mackinac Bridge Sunset

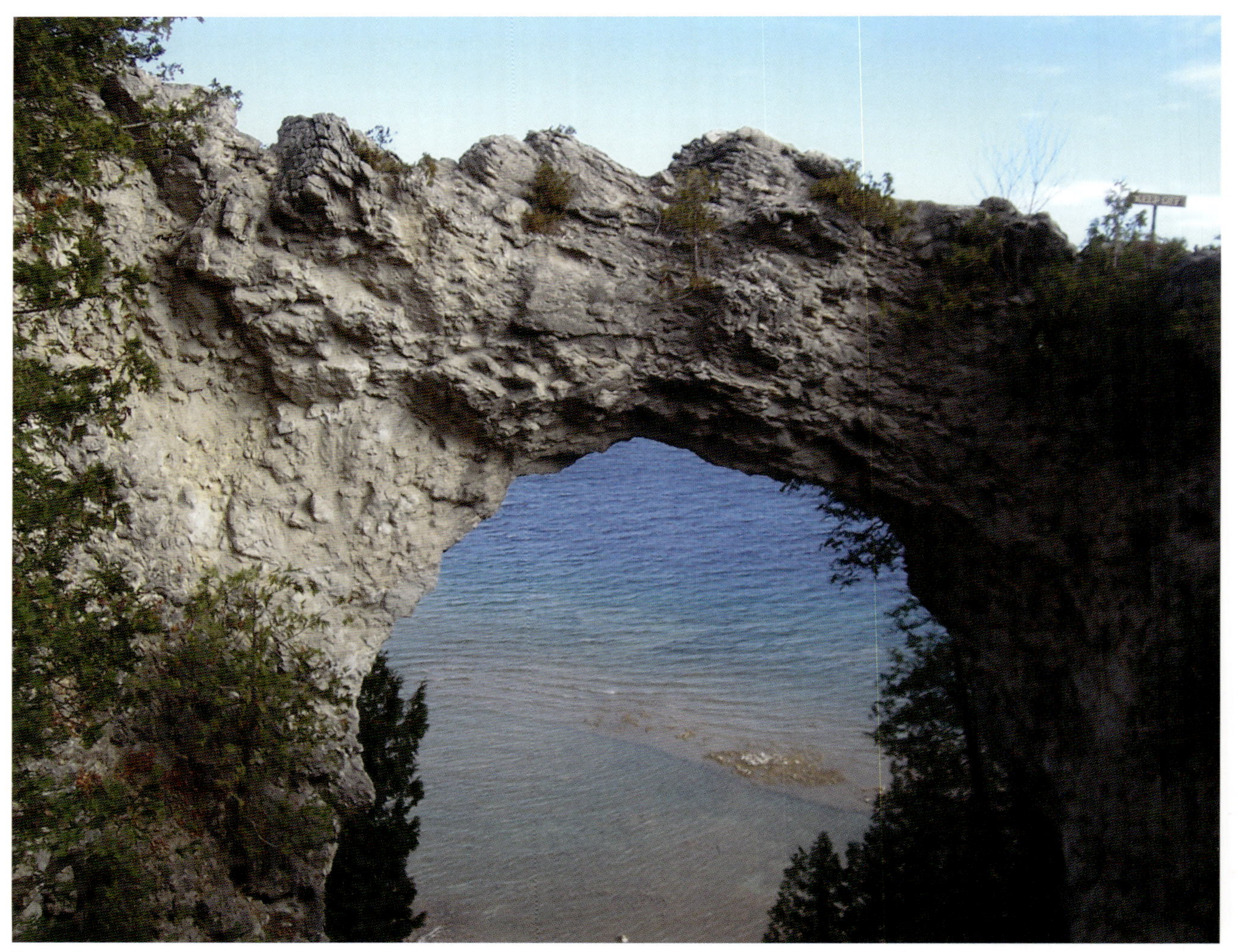

Barb Jenkins

Arch Rock, Mackinac Island

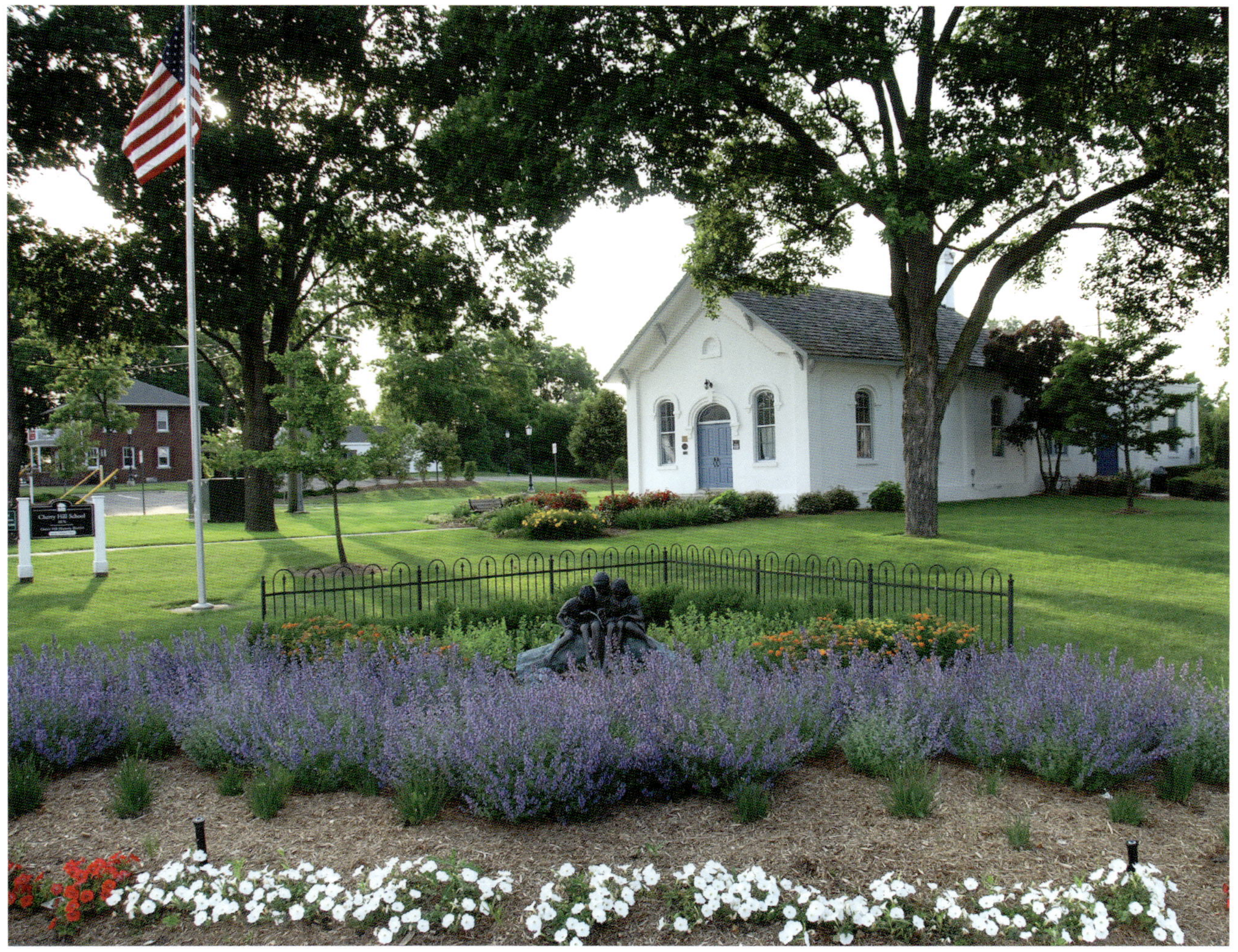

Charles D. Mott

Cherry Hill School, Canton

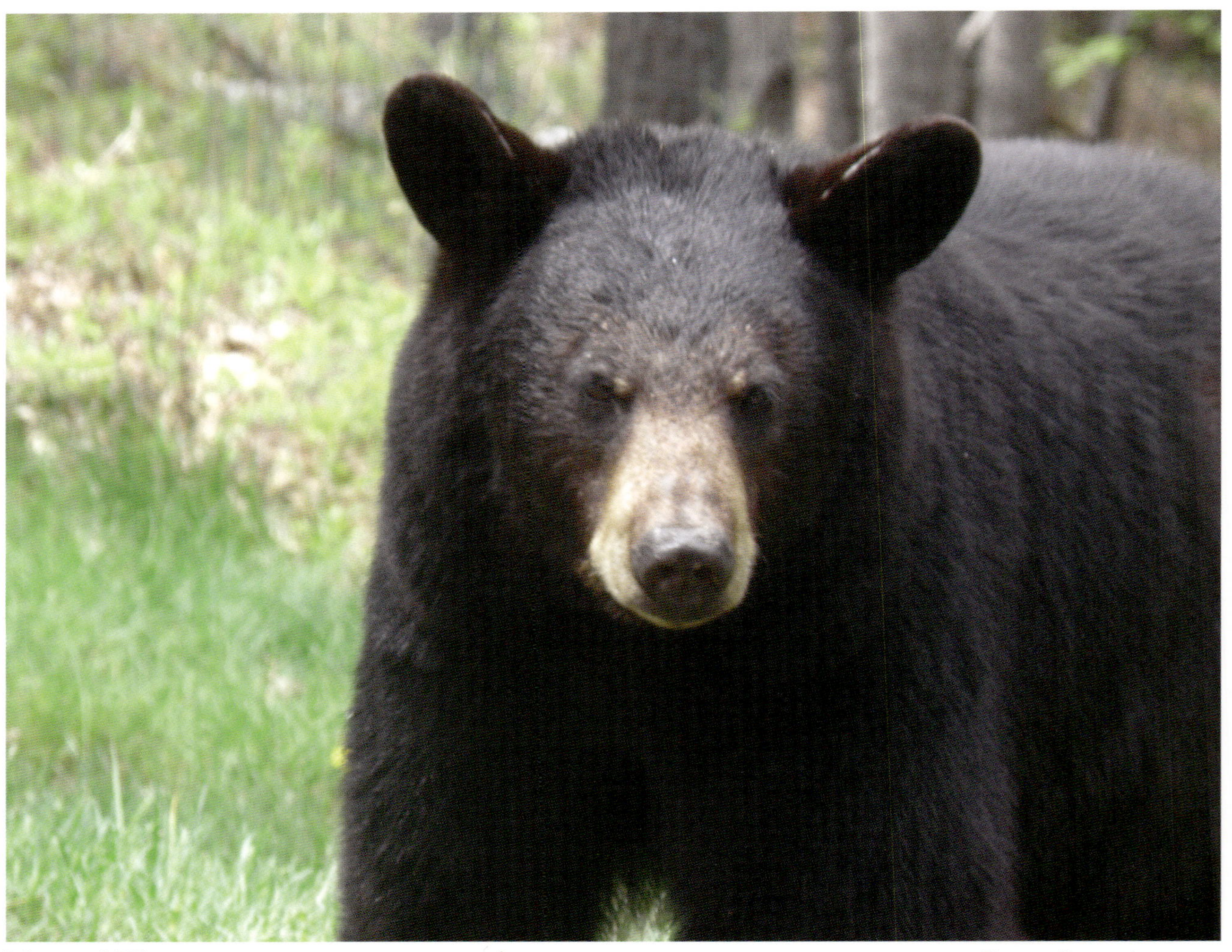

Marion J. Wood — Black Bear, Atlanta

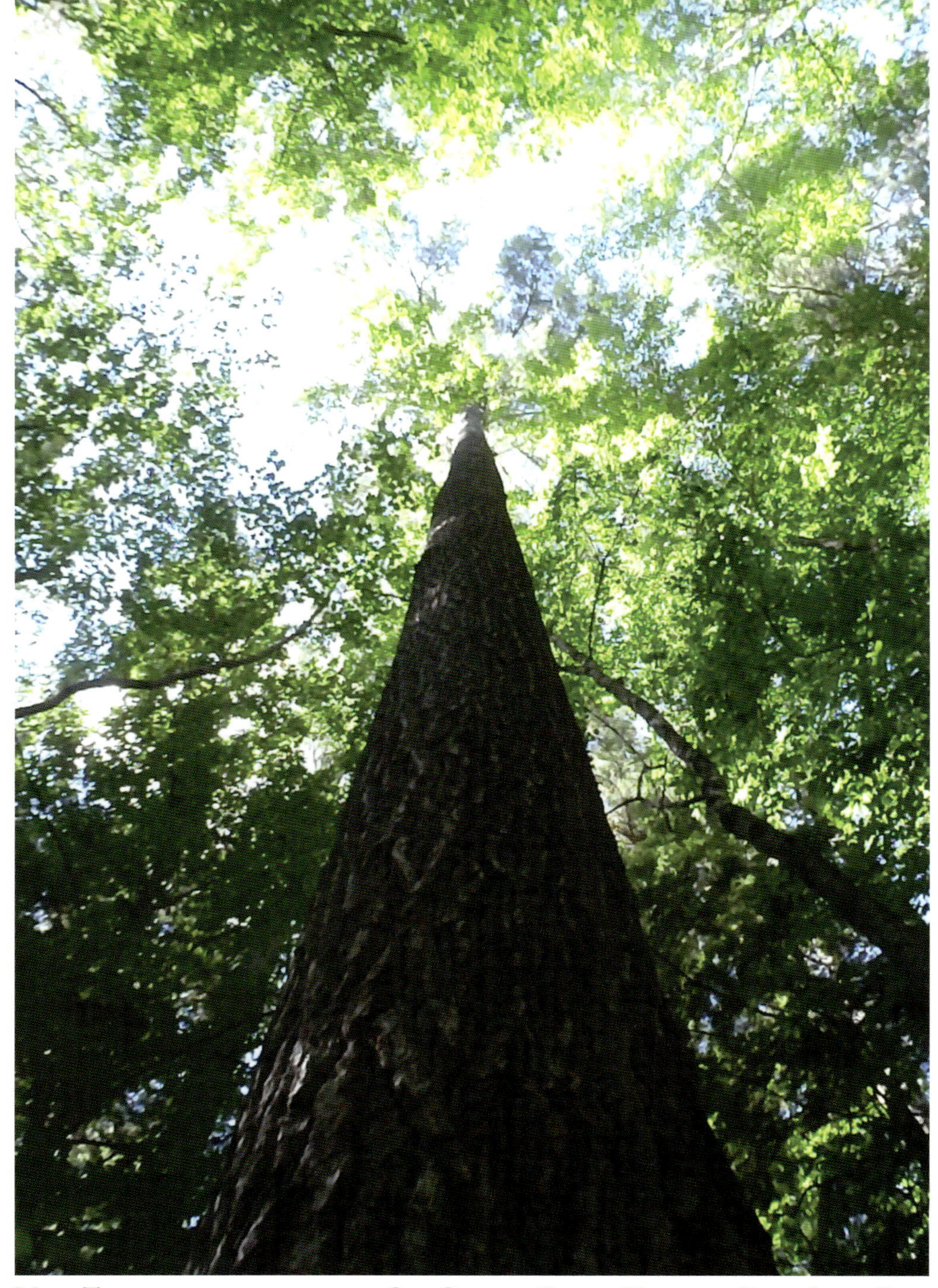

Mark Taylor — Old Growth Forest, Hartwick Pines State Park

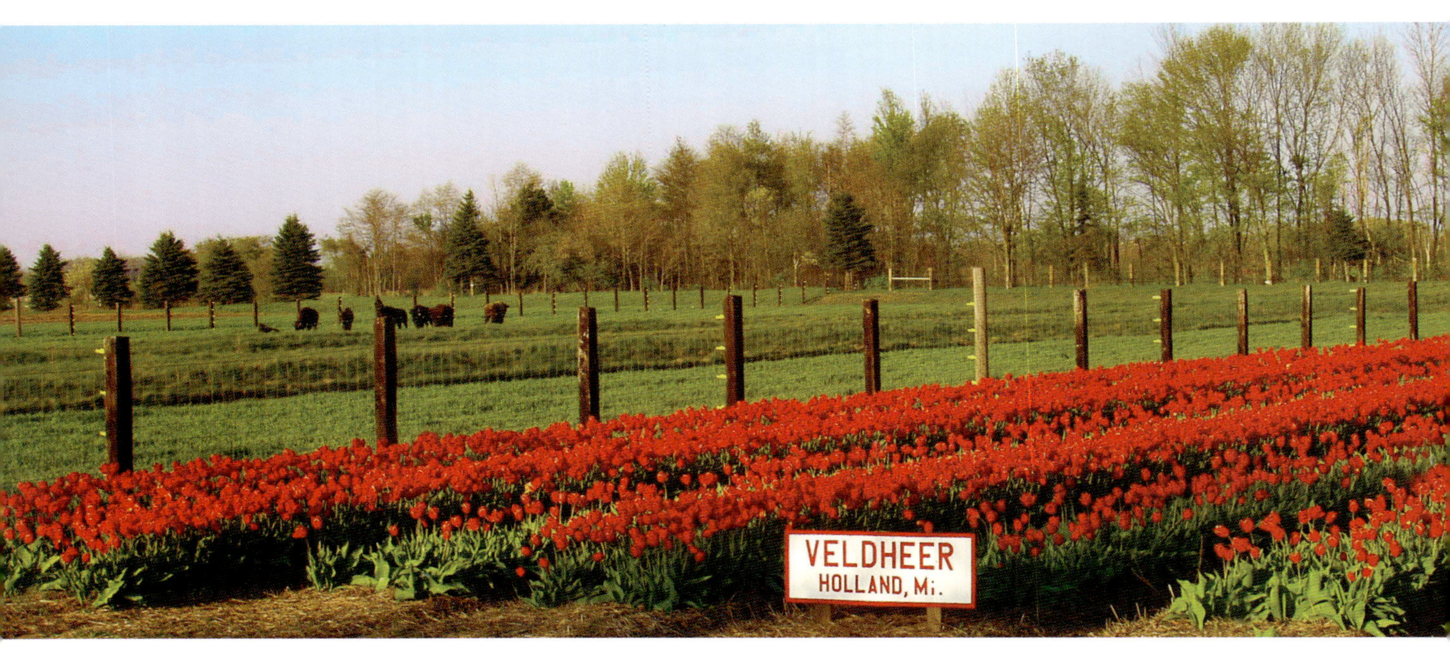

Valerie van Heest

Veldeer Tulips, Holland

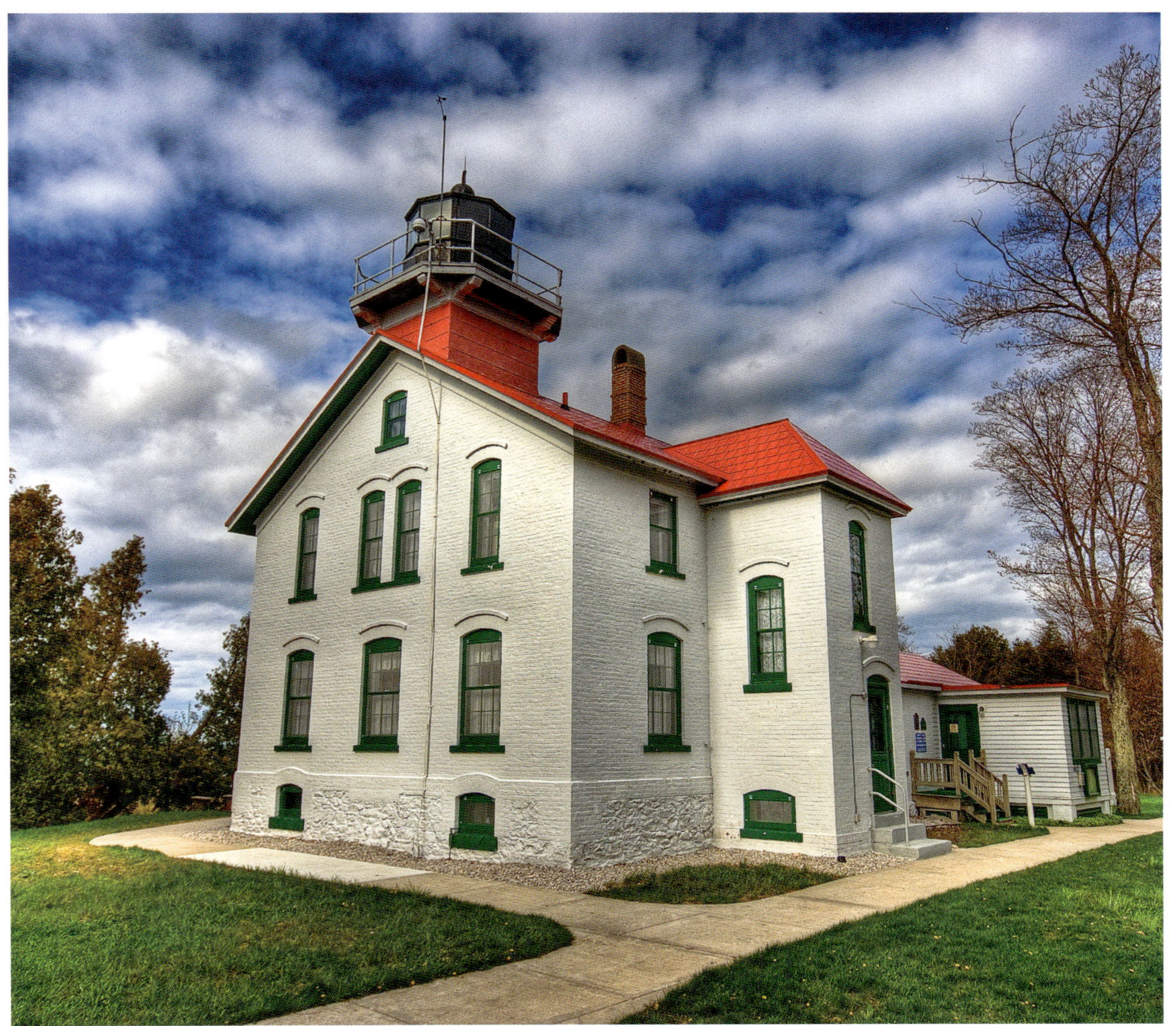

Dennis H. Guthrie

Grand Traverse Lighthouse, Leelanau State Park

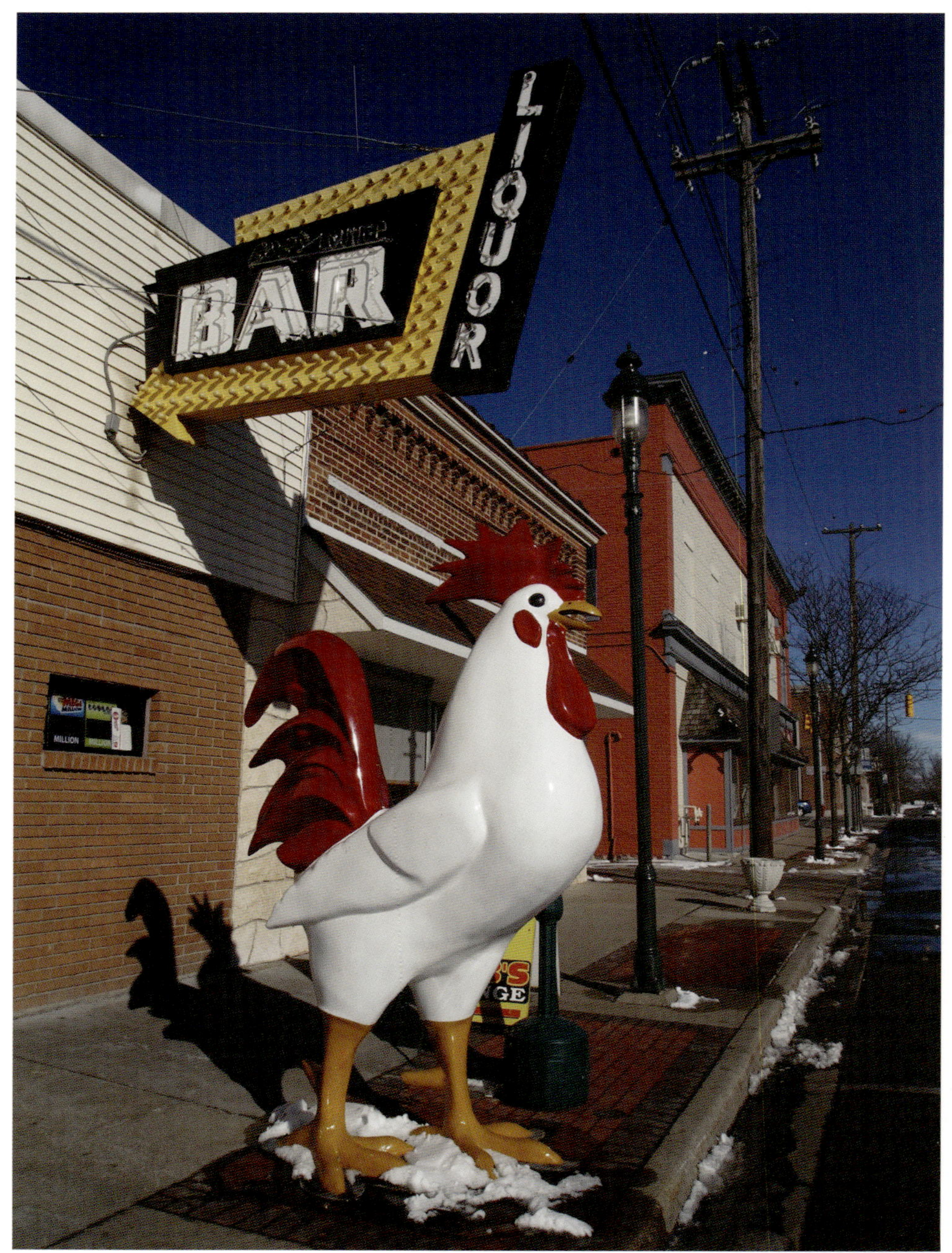

Rebecca Allen

The Big Rooster, Clare

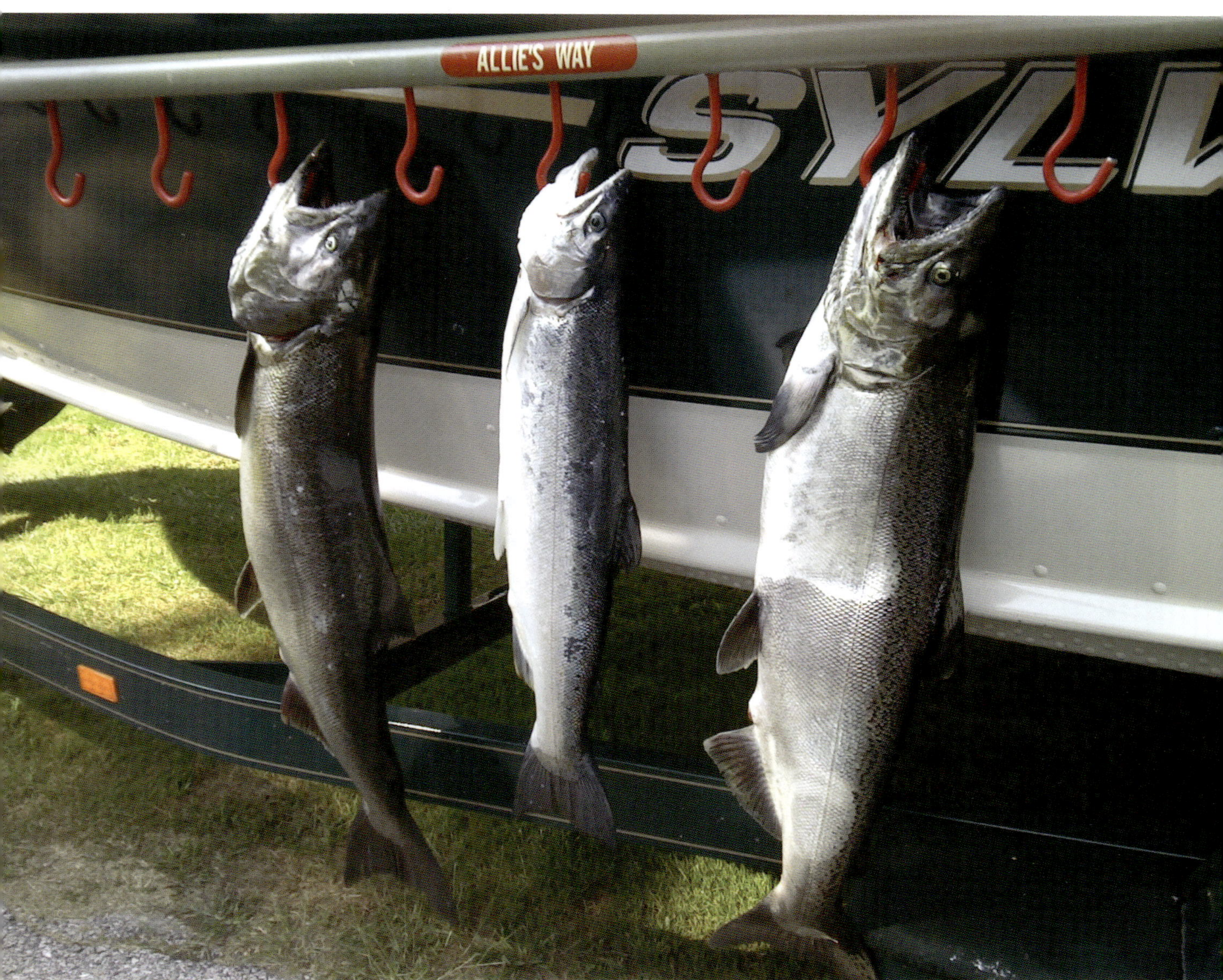

Becky Kilpatrick

Successful Day Salmon Fishing, Onekama

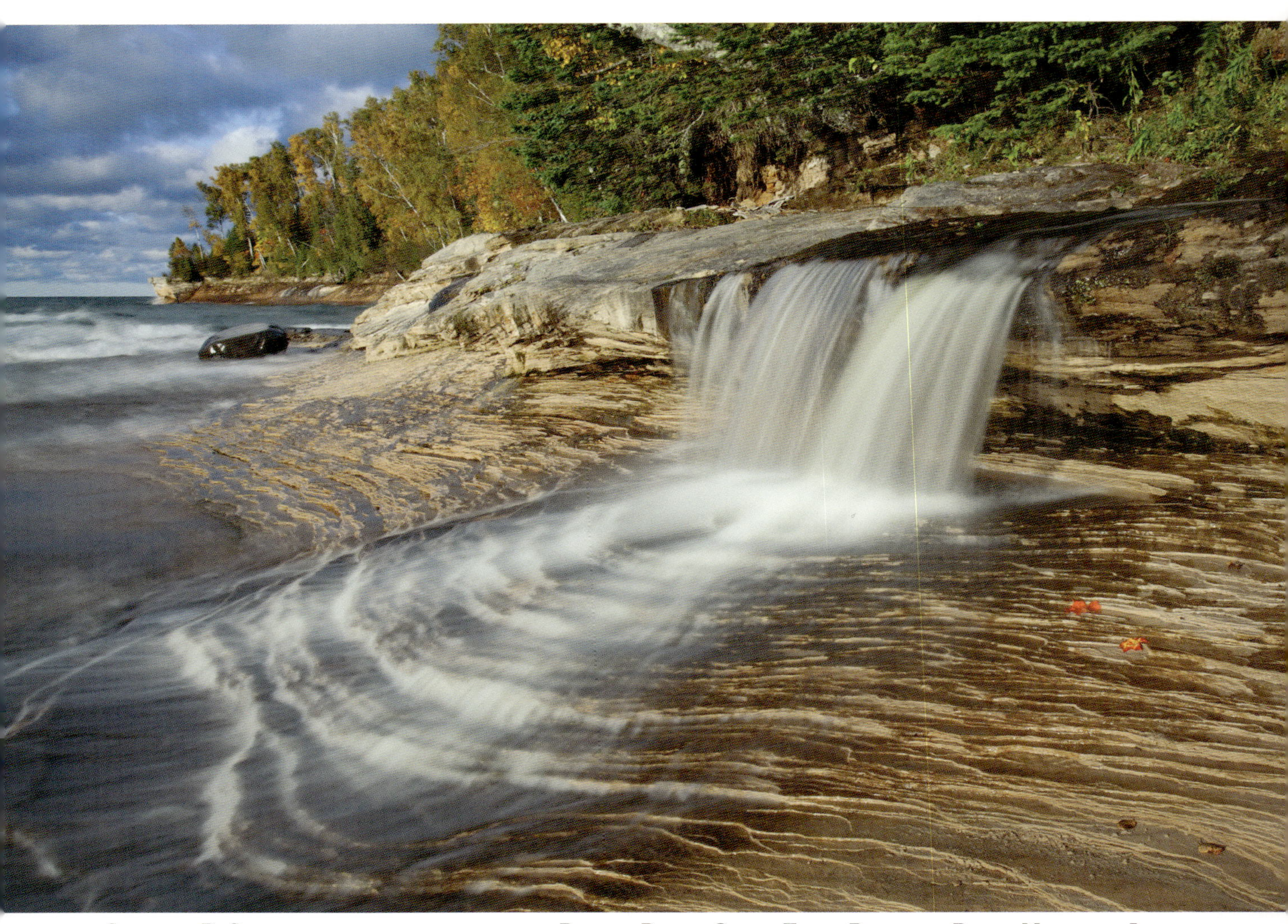

Stephen R. Sage

Potato Patch Creek Falls, Pictured Rocks National Lakeshore

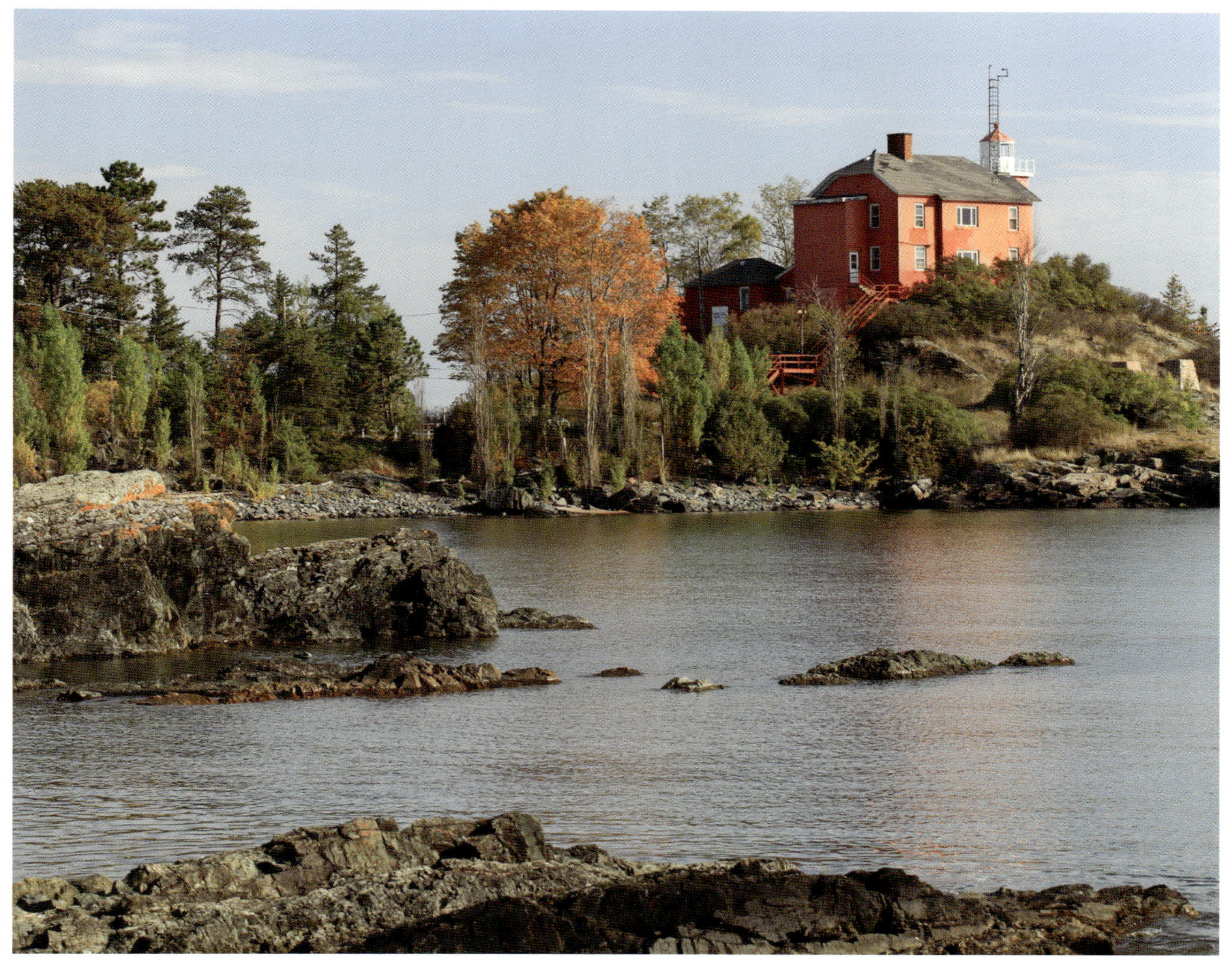

Julien Brasseur

Marquette Harbor Light, Marquette

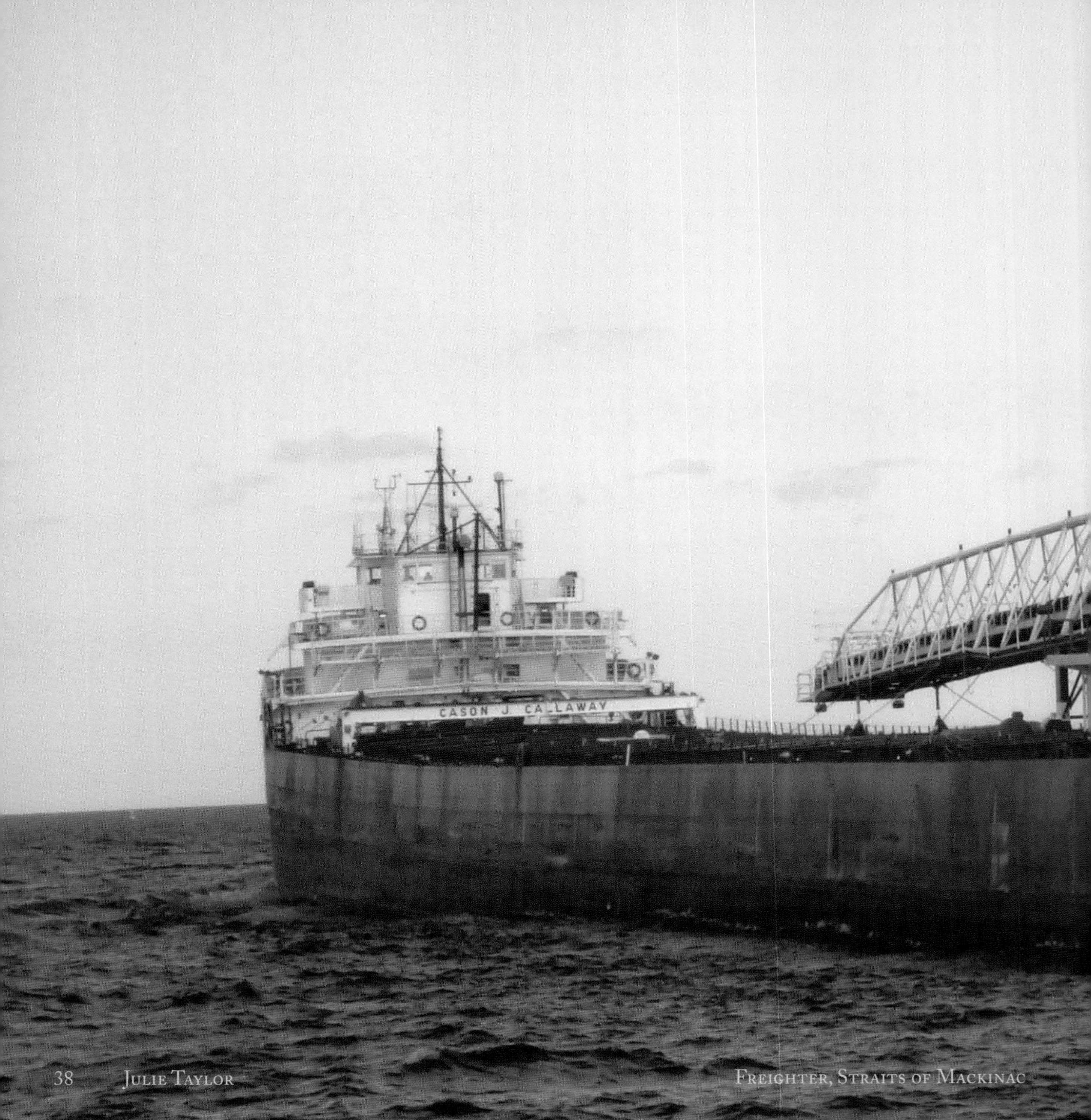

Freighter, Straits of Mackinac

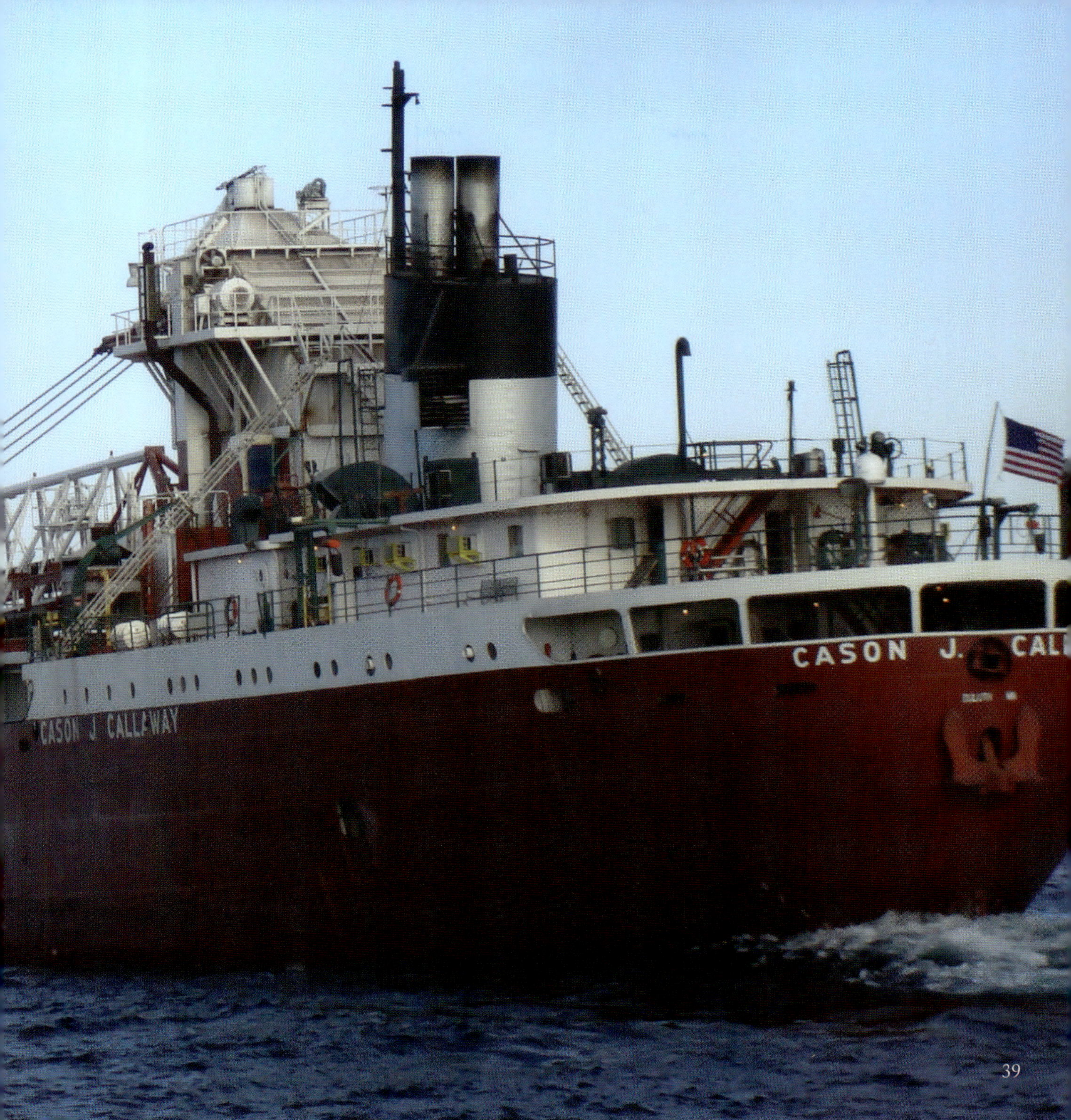
CASON J CALLAWAY
CASON J. CAL

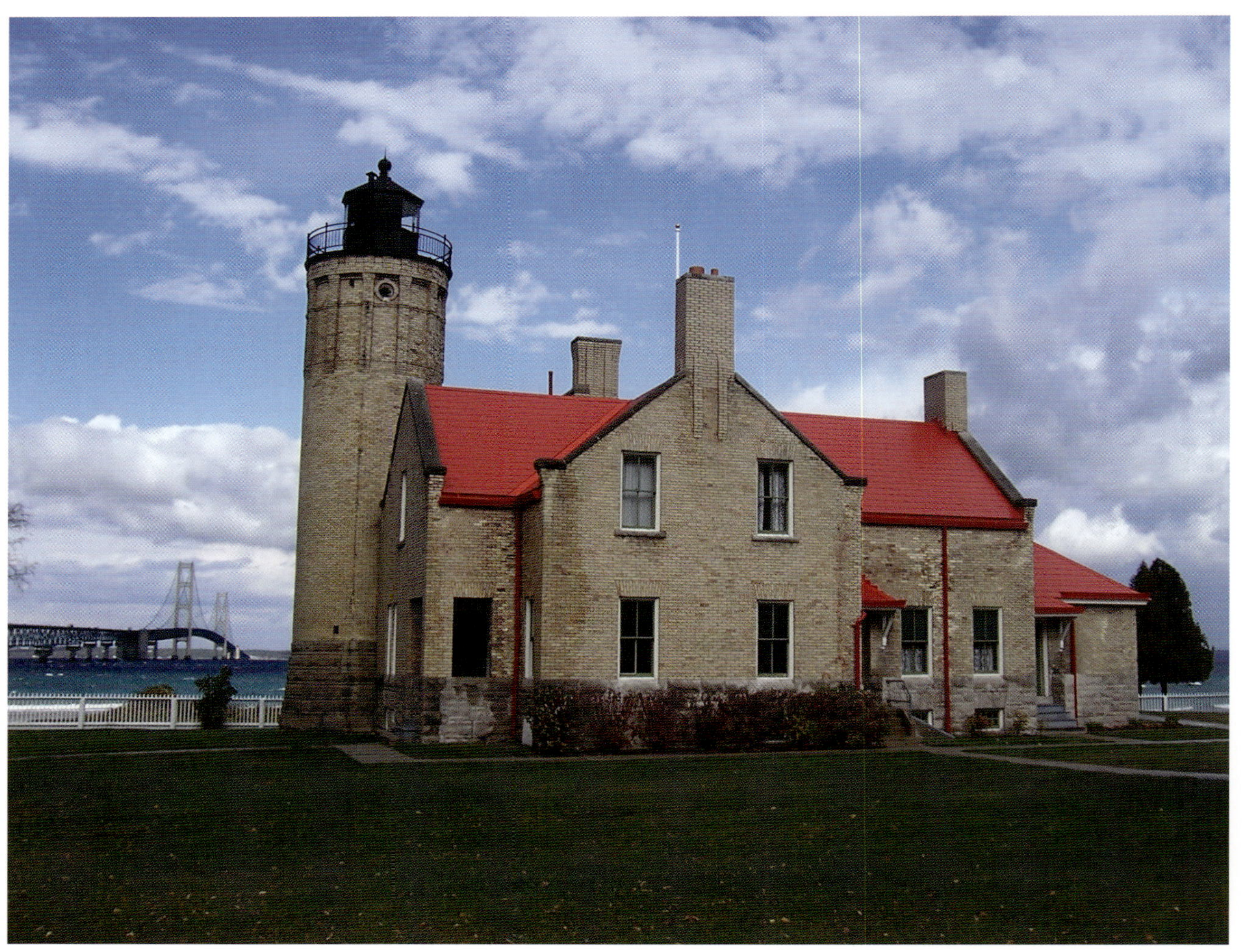

Barb Jenkins

Old Mackinac Point Lighthouse, Mackinaw City

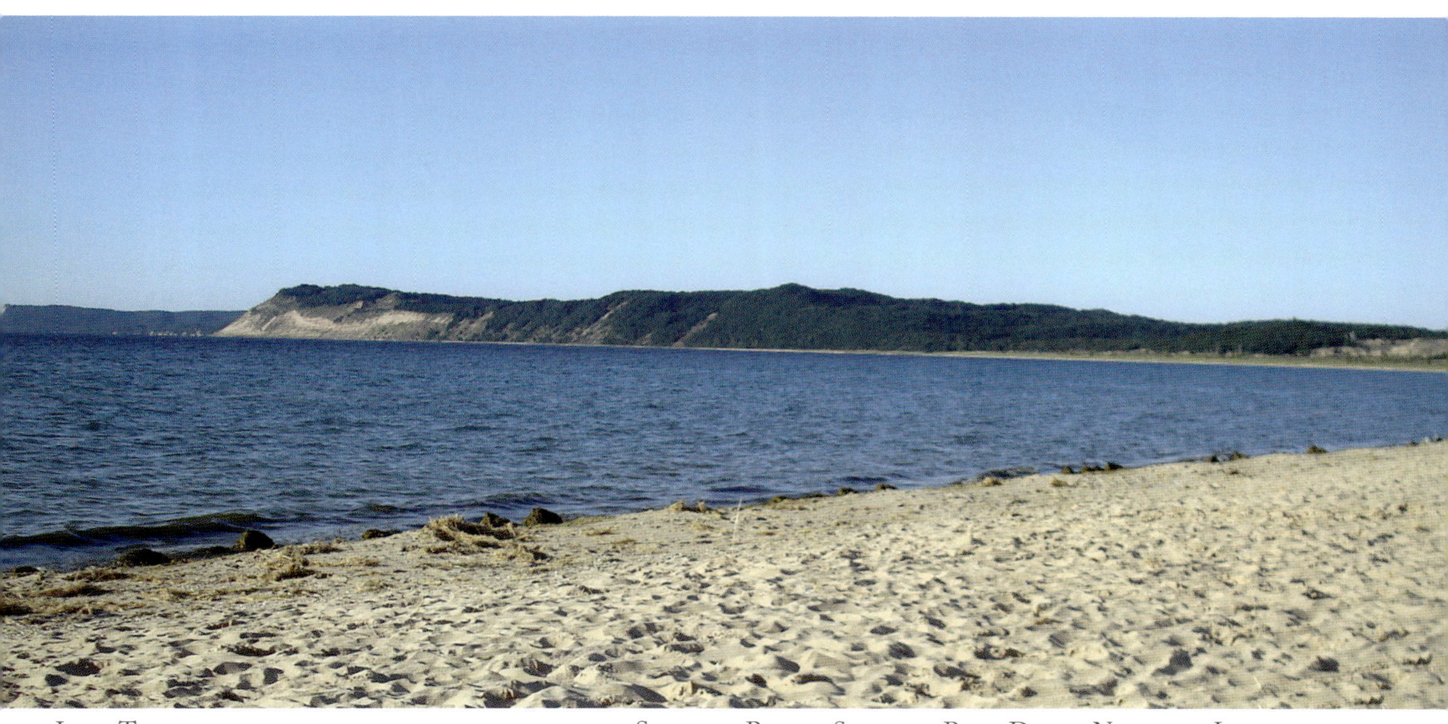

Julie Taylor Sleeping Beach, Sleeping Bear Dunes National Lakeshore

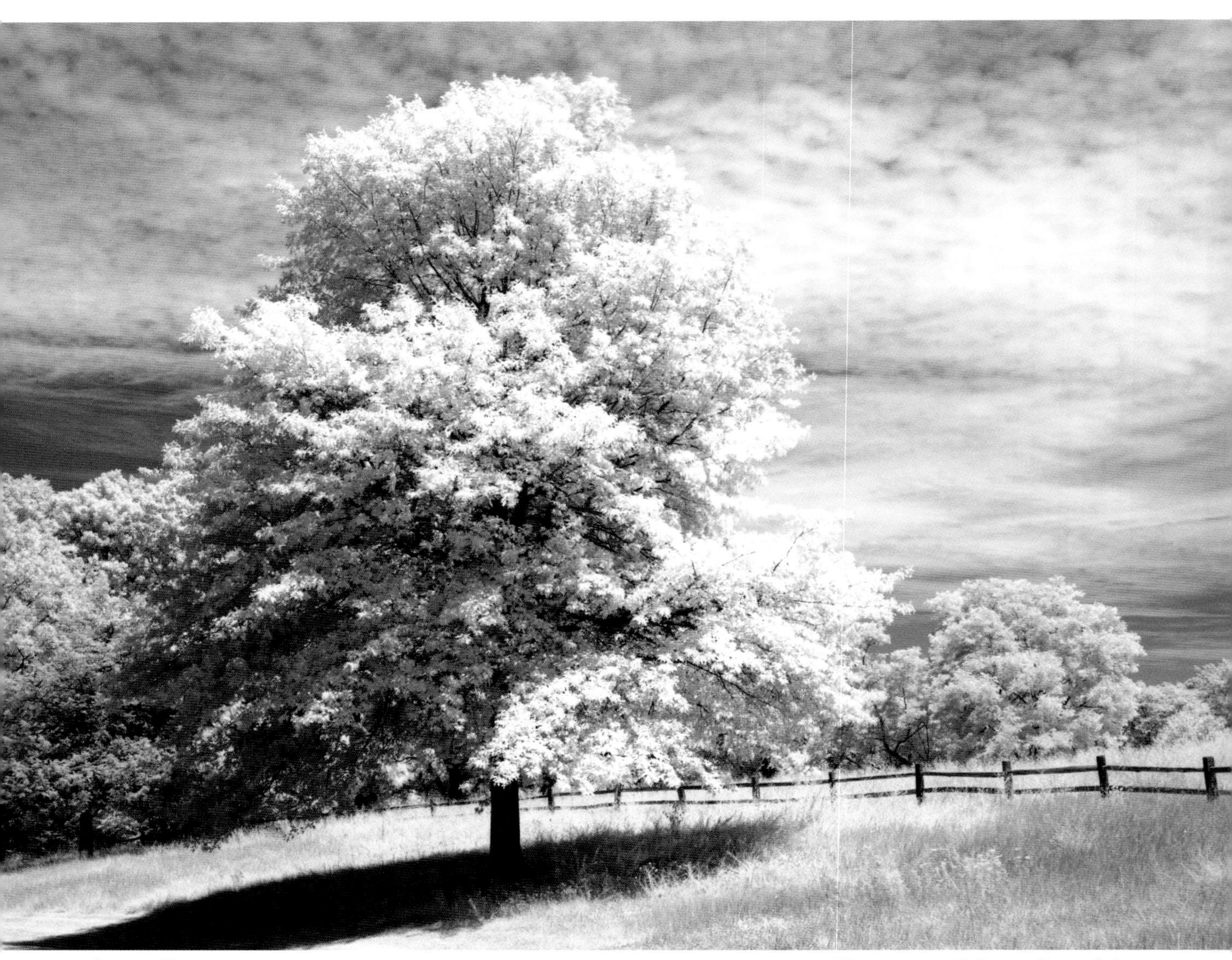

Scott Nicholson Kensington Metro Park, Milford

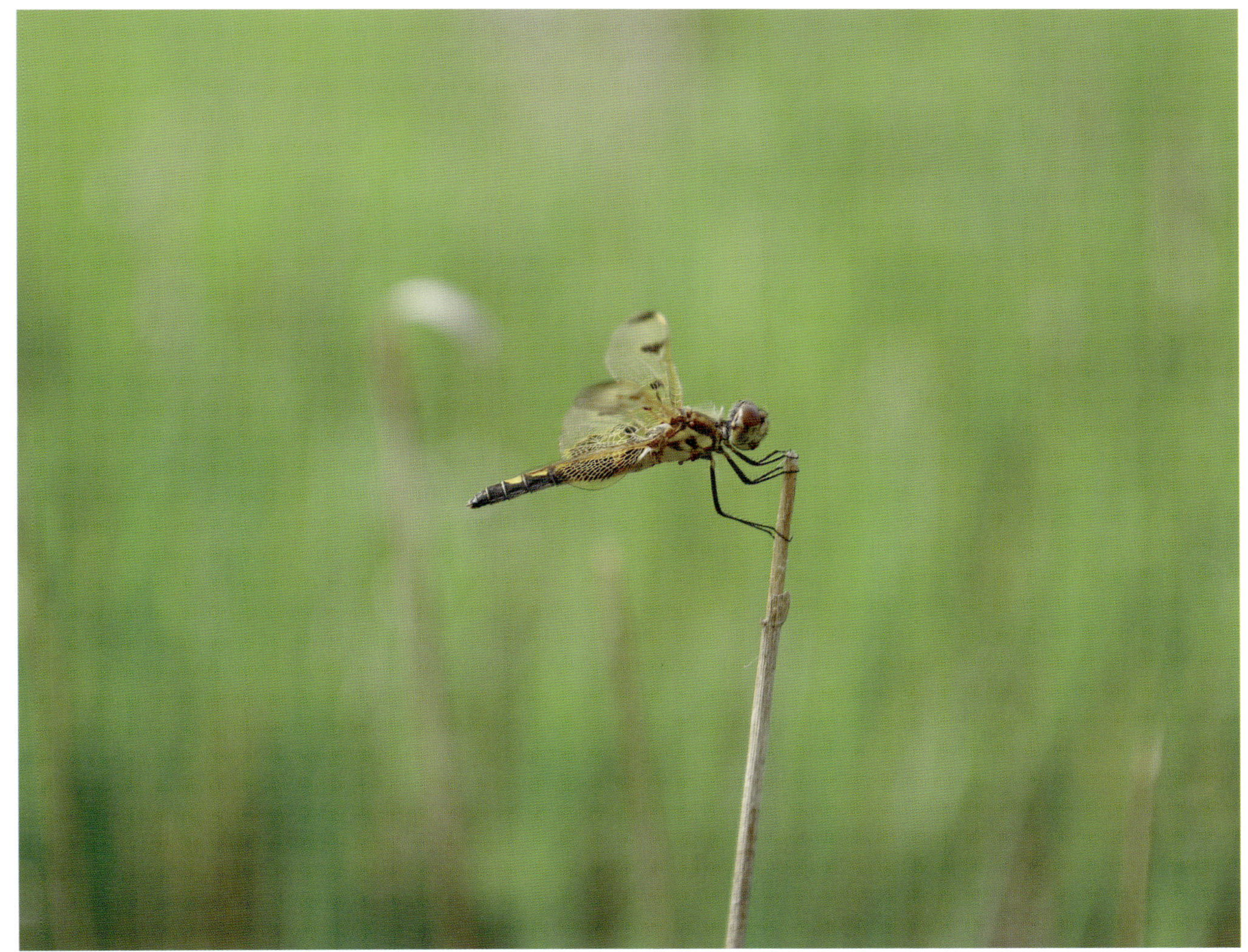

Rebecca Allen — Hanging on to Summer, Laingsburg

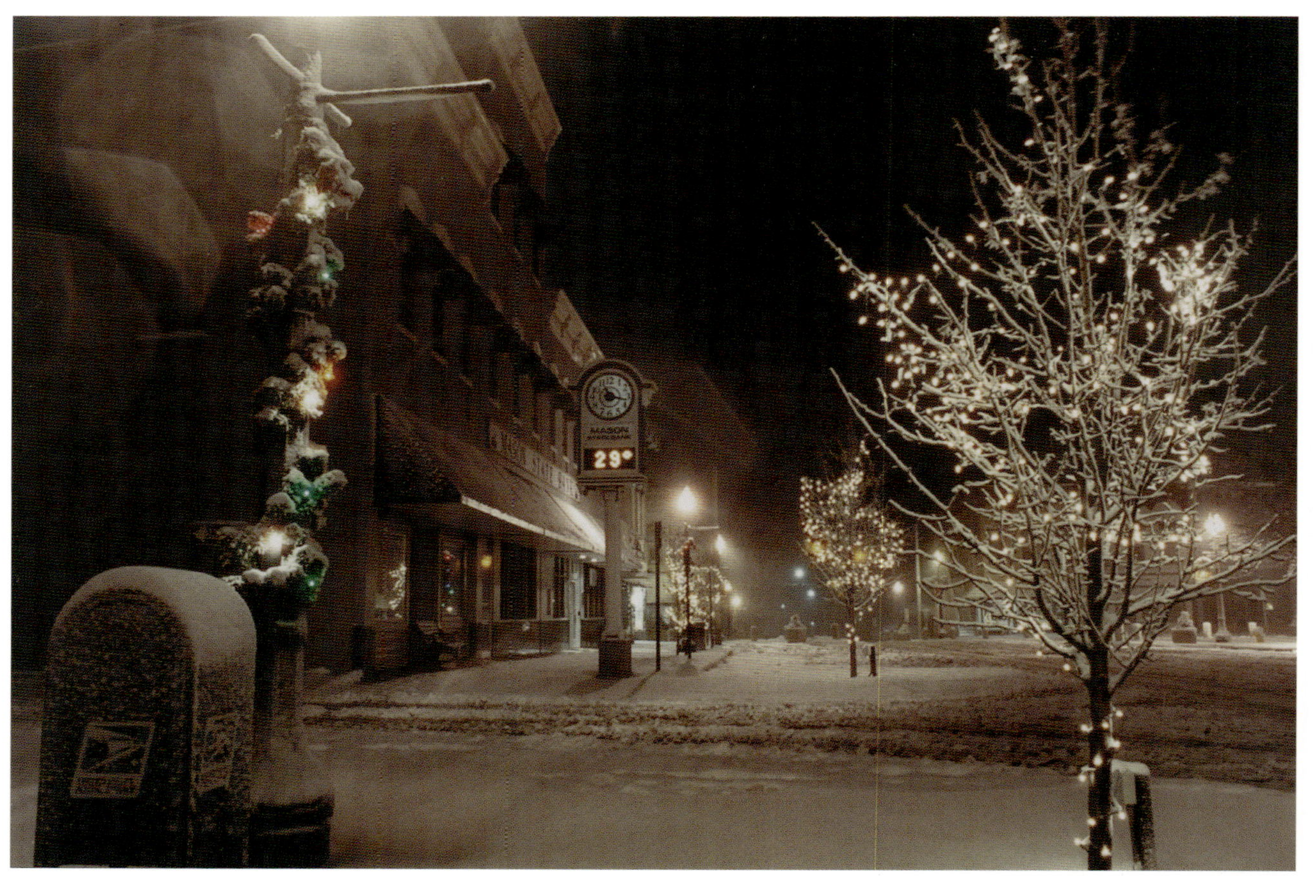

LOREN S. SHATTUCK

DOWNTOWN MASON

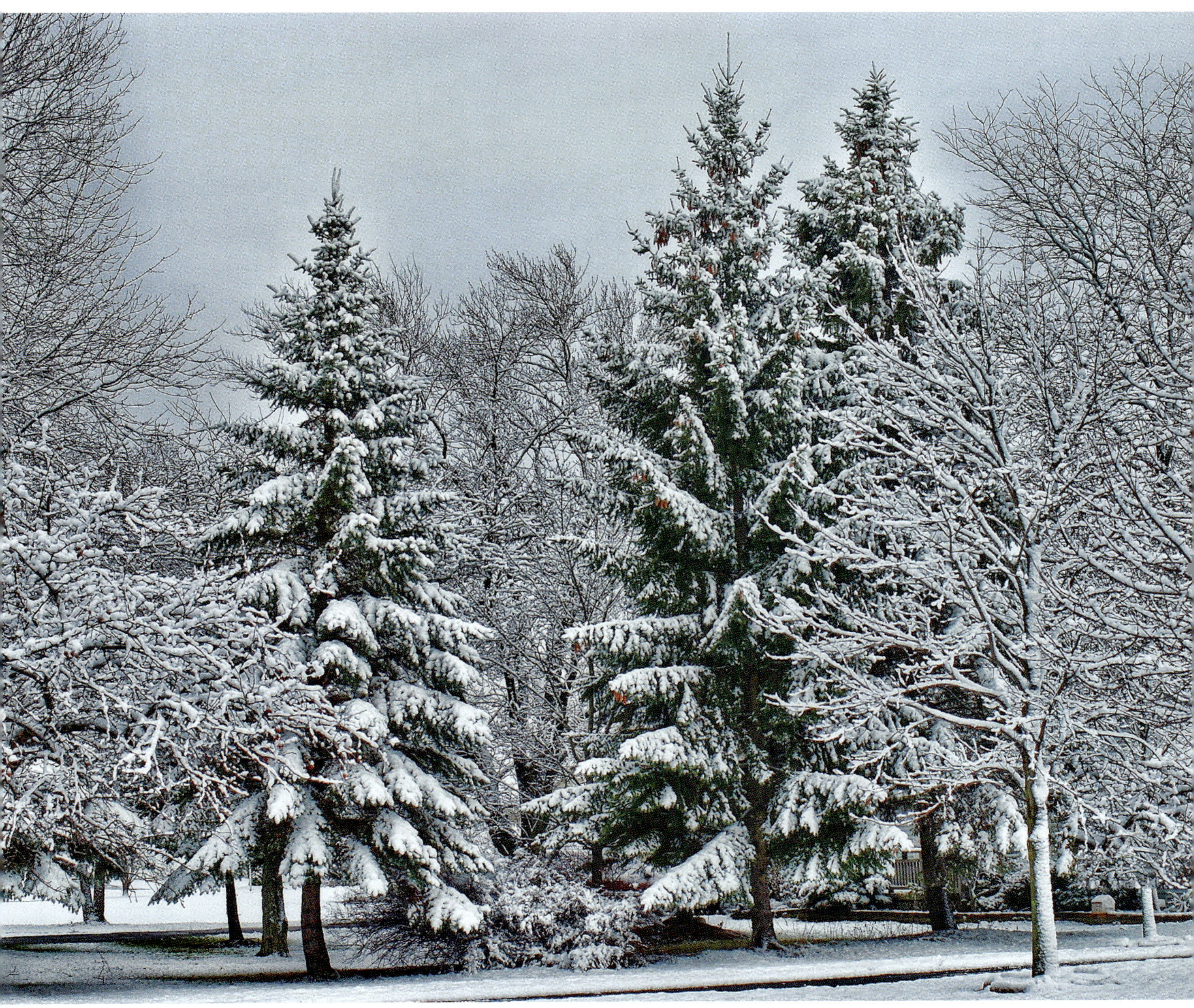

CHARLES D. MOTT

FRONT YARD IN WINTER, CANTON

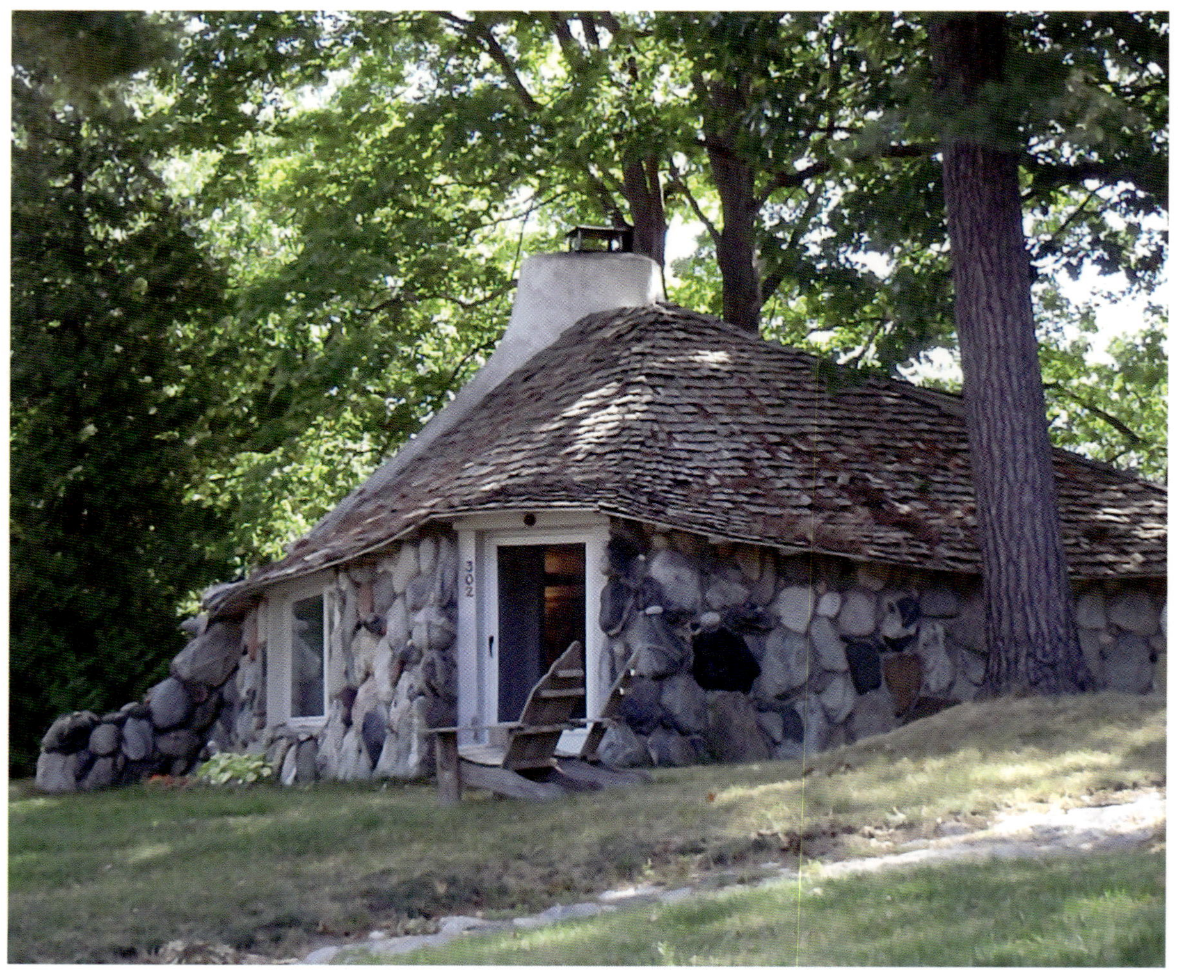

Mark Taylor — Mushroom House, Charlevoix

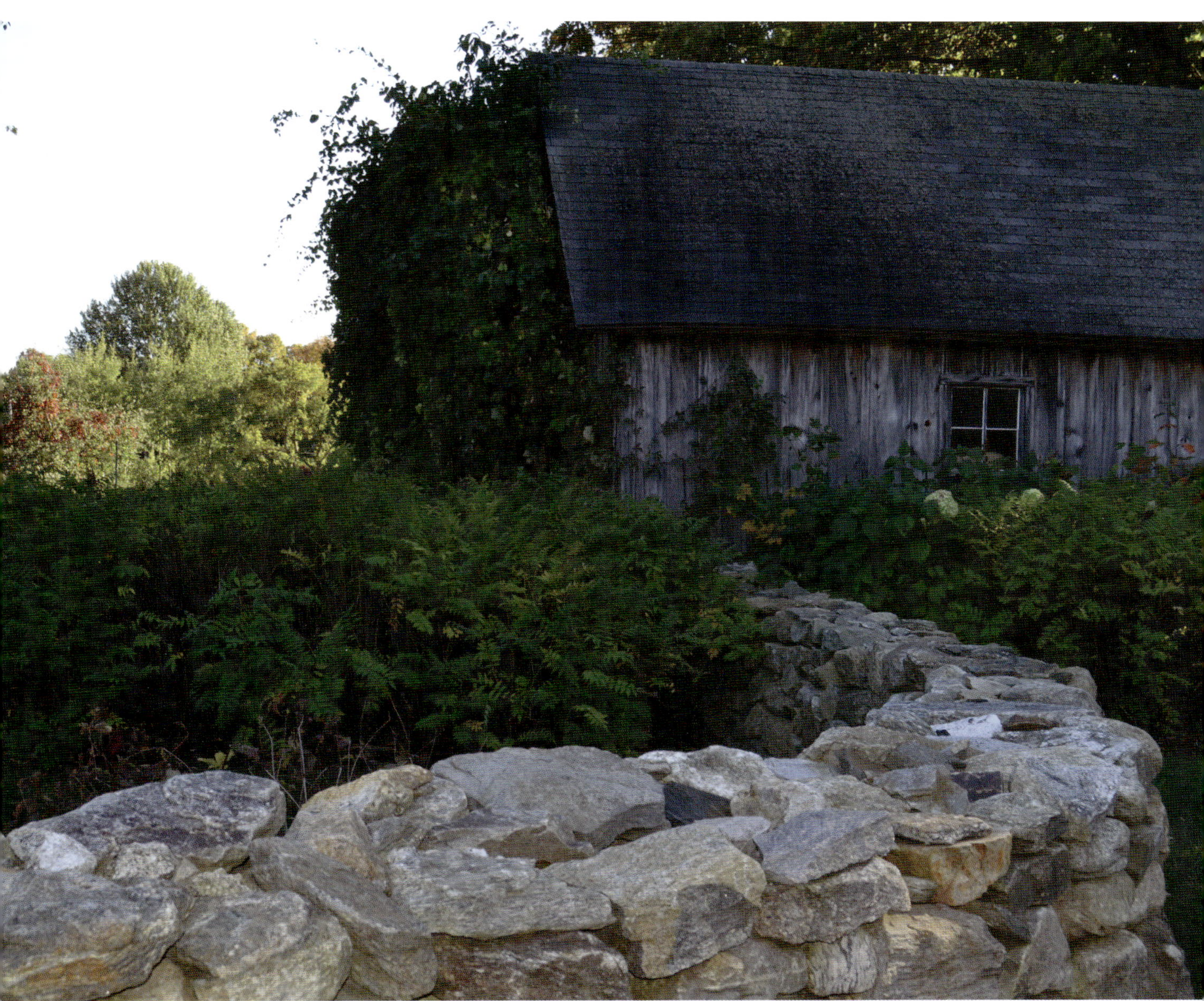

Brandy L. Crump

The Old Woodshed, Harbor Springs

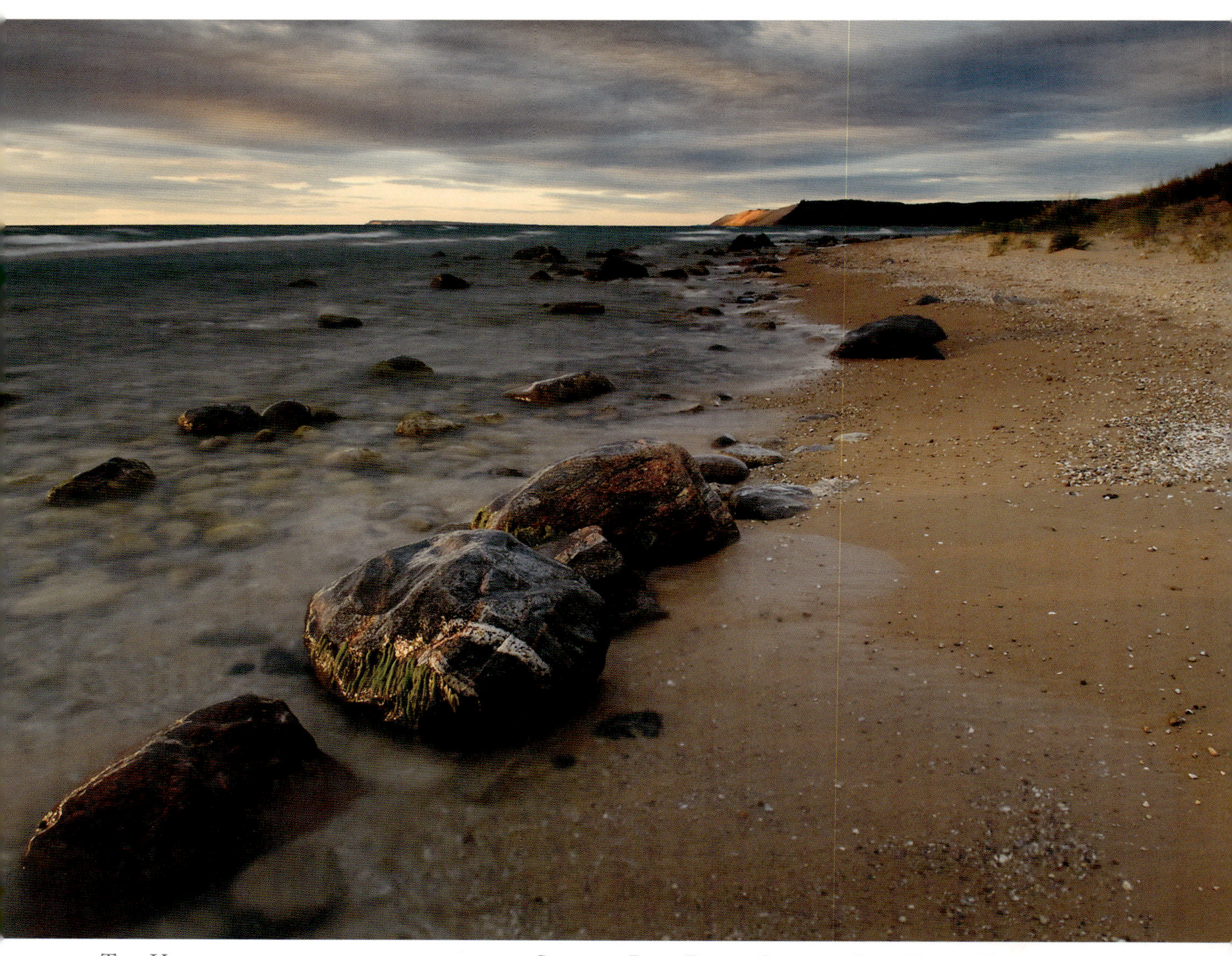

Tom Haxby Sleeping Bear Dunes, Sleeping Bear Dunes National Lakeshore

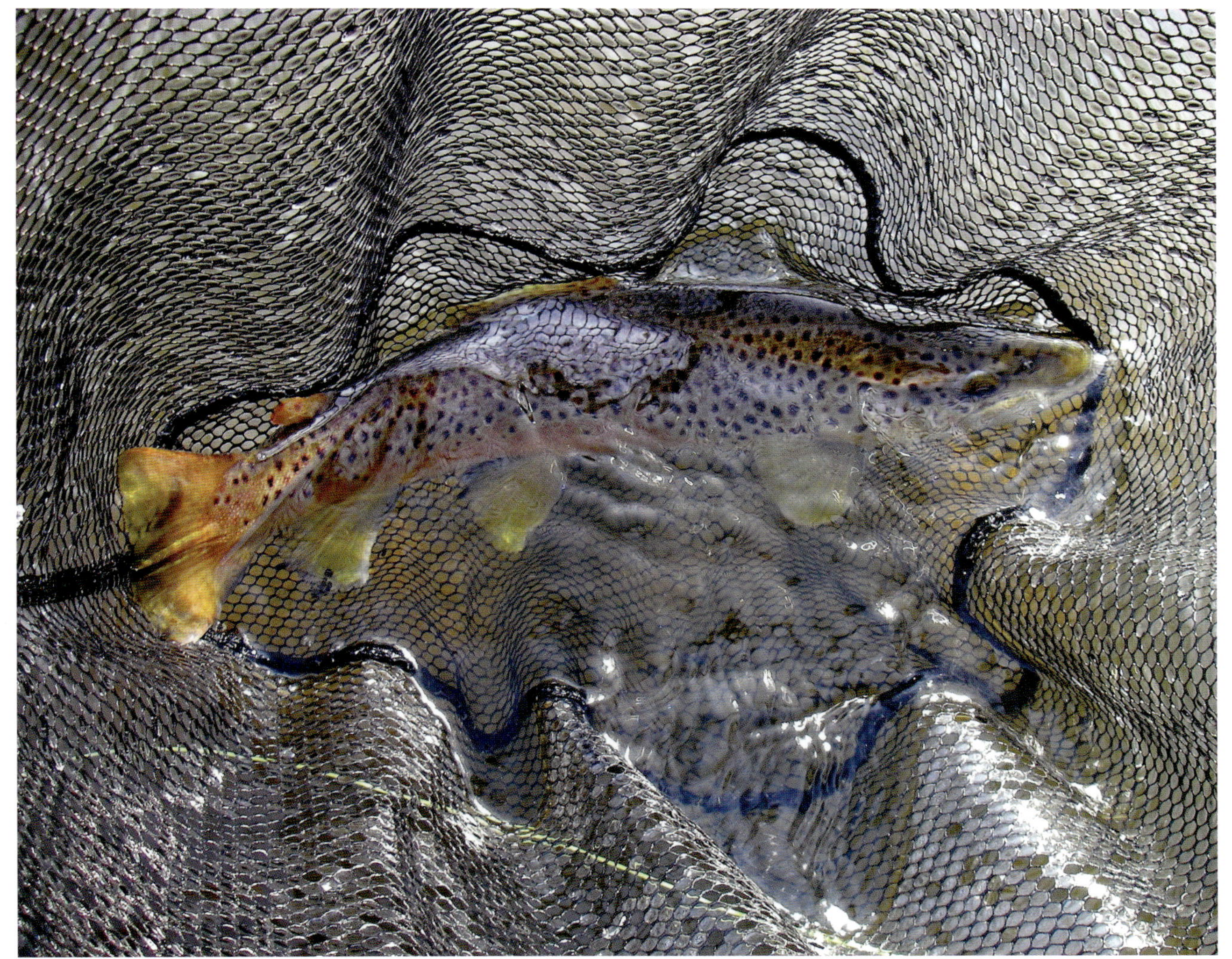

Rebecca Allen

Netted Brown Trout, Ionia County

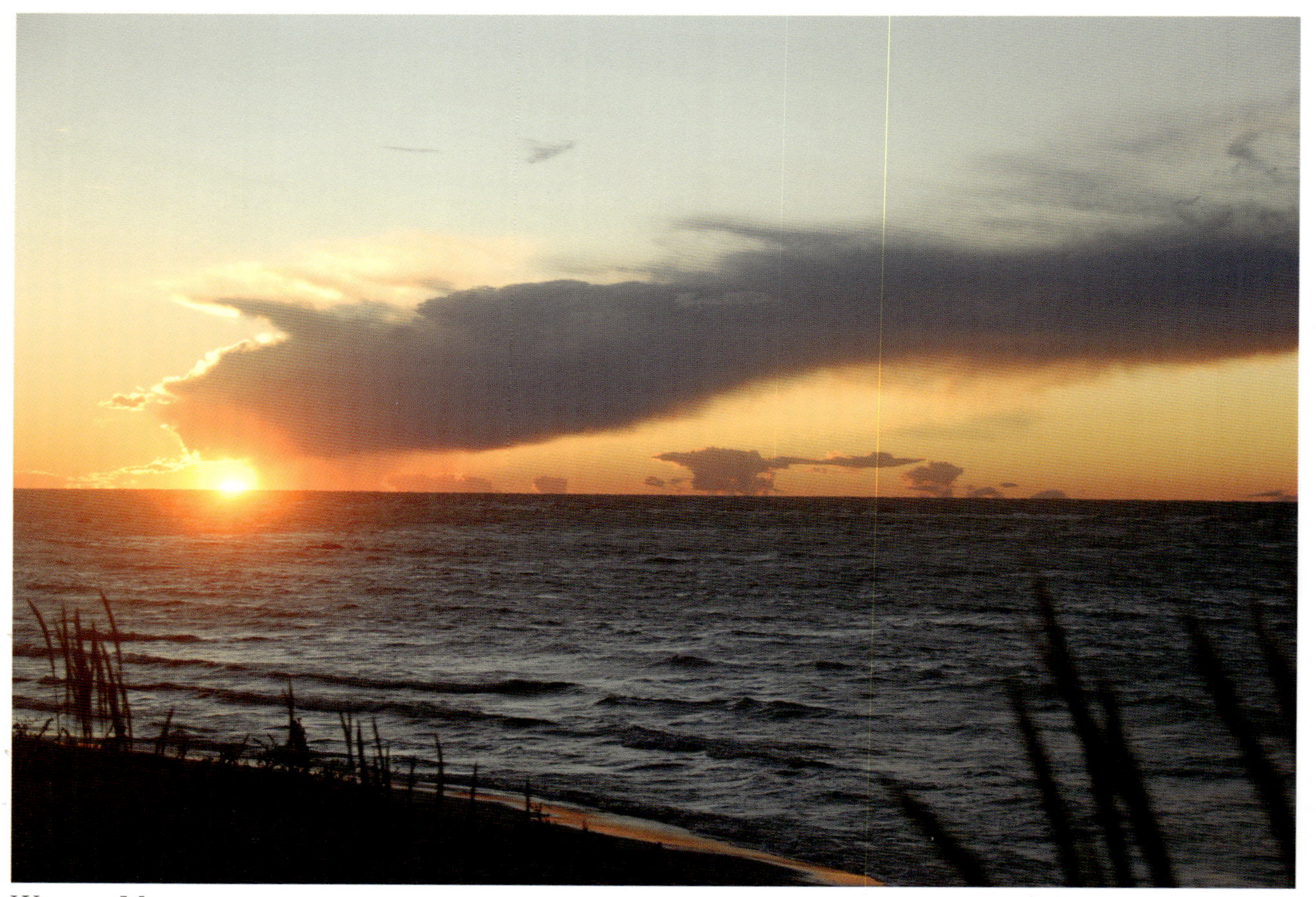

William Mayes — Sunset, Port Austin

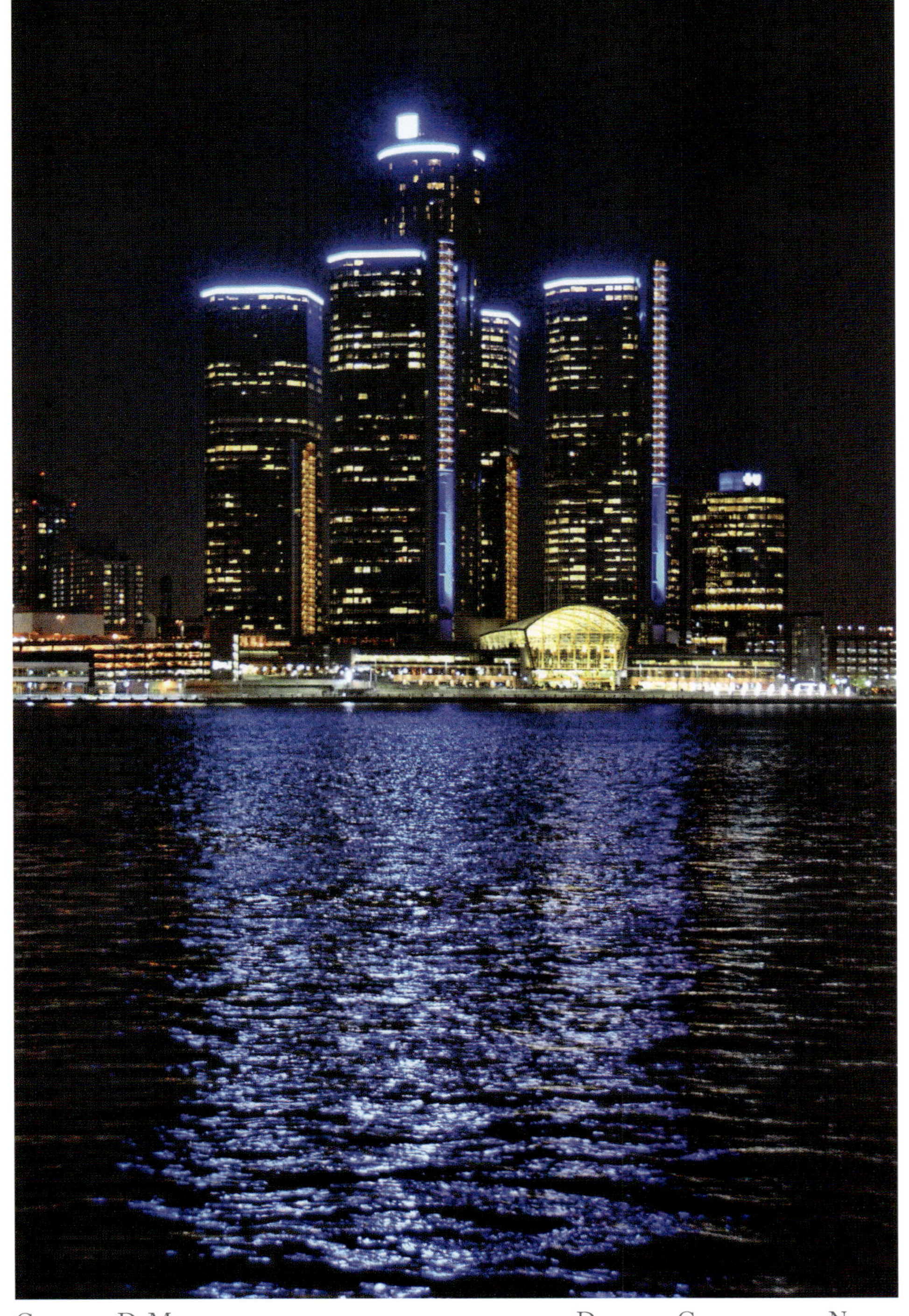

Charles D. Mott — Detroit Cityscape at Night

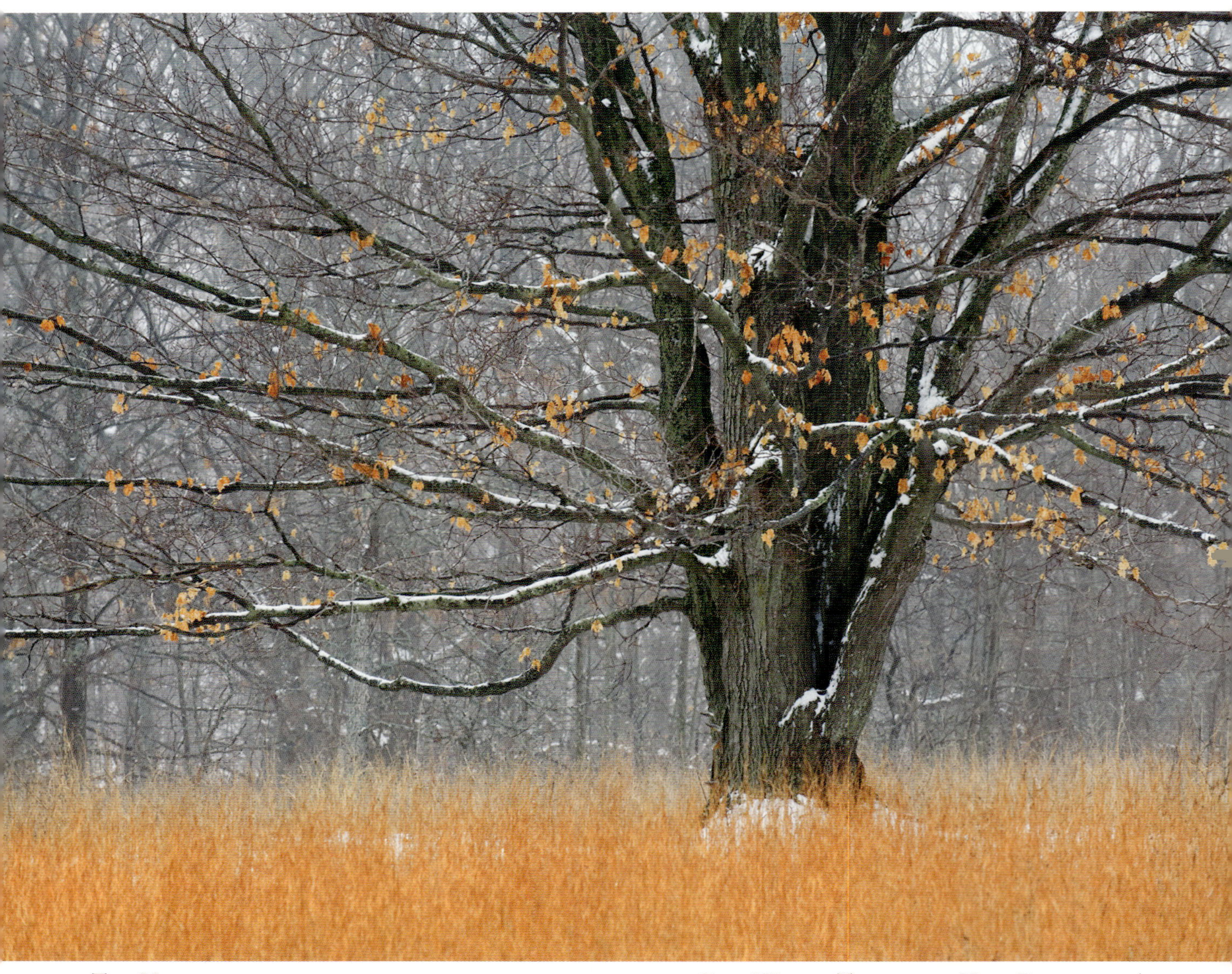

Tom Haxby

Fall-Winter Transition, High Rollaways Area

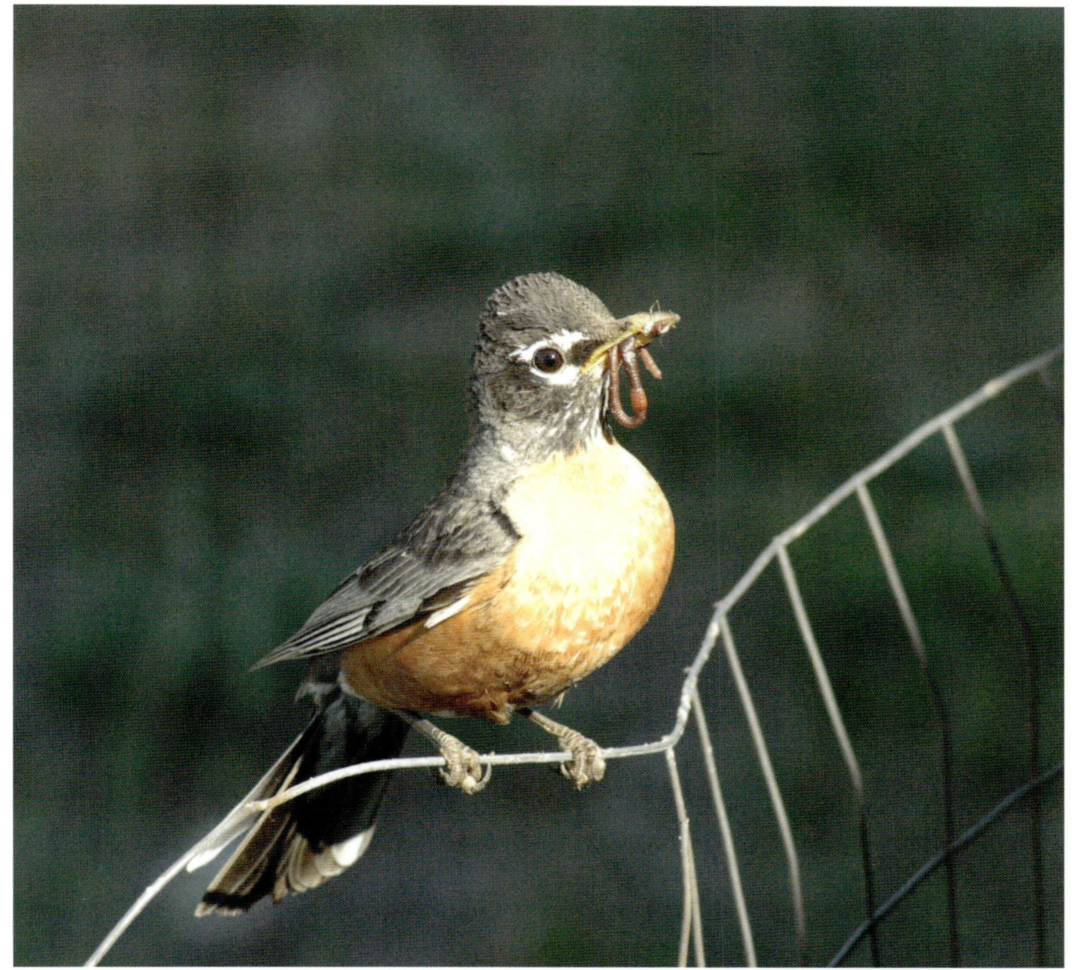

Dove Day Juvenile Robin, Petoskey

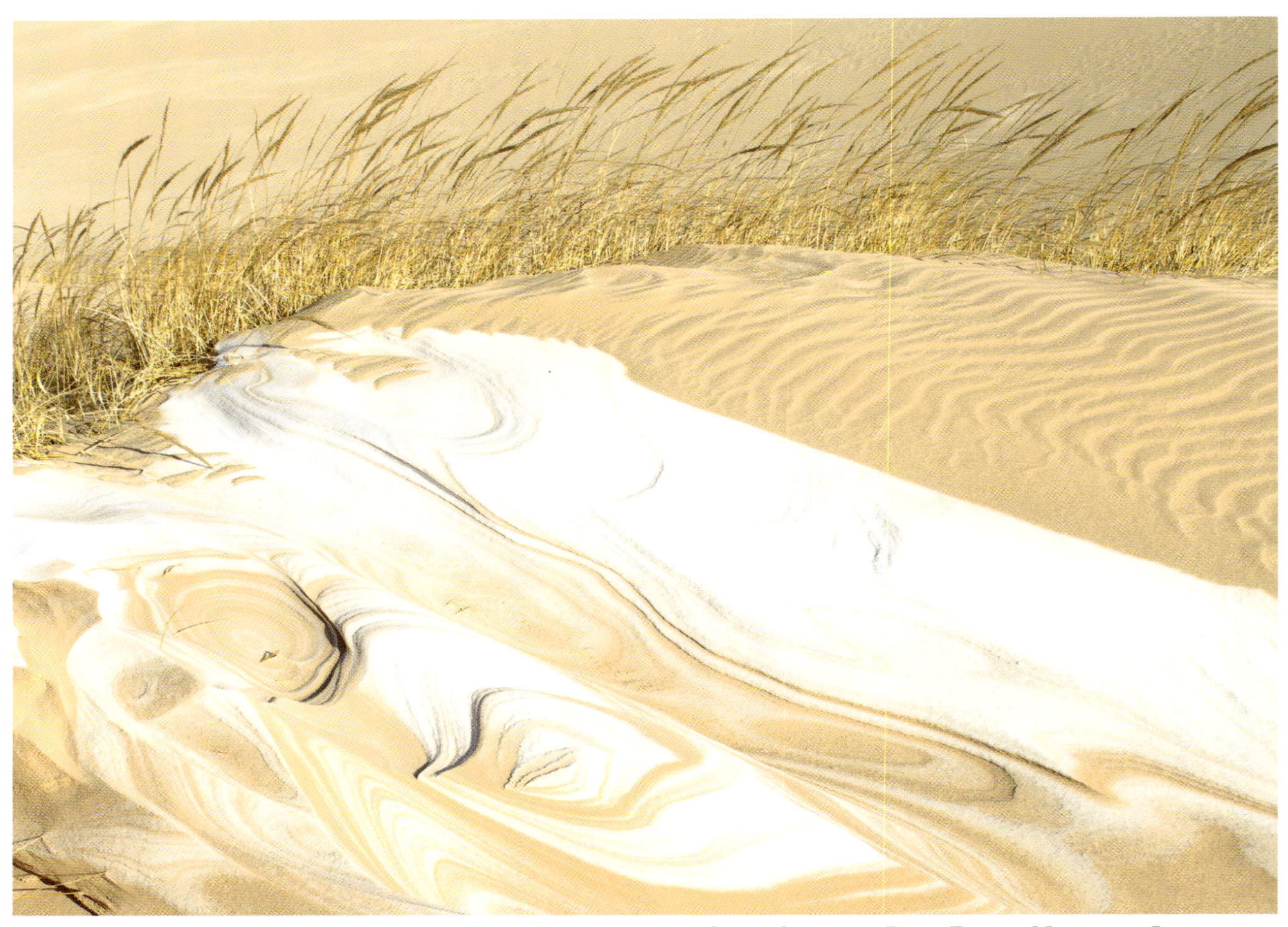

John Lloyd — Snow Swirled with Sand, Sleeping Bear Dunes National Lakeshore

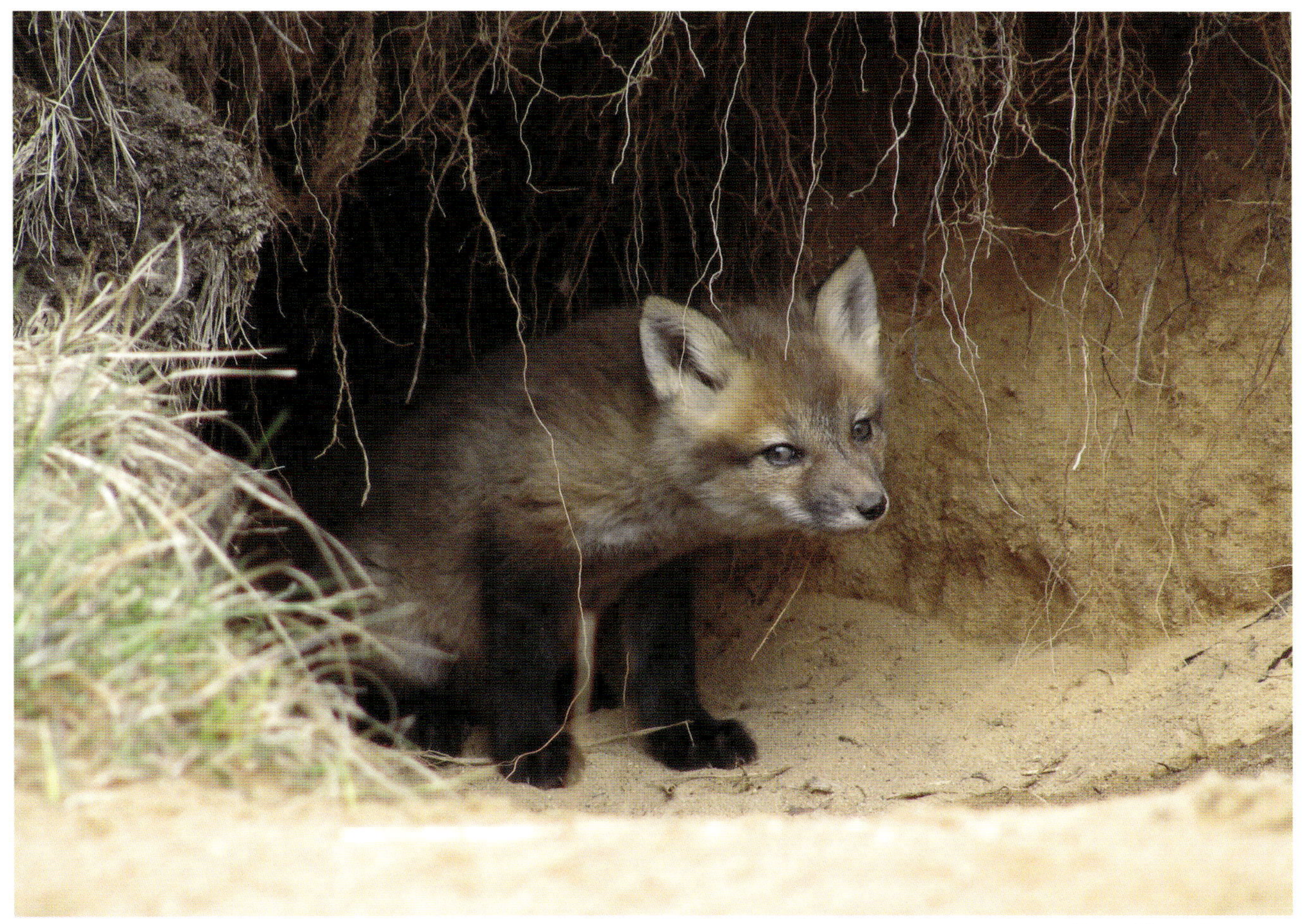

Webster Wood Baby Fox, Atlanta

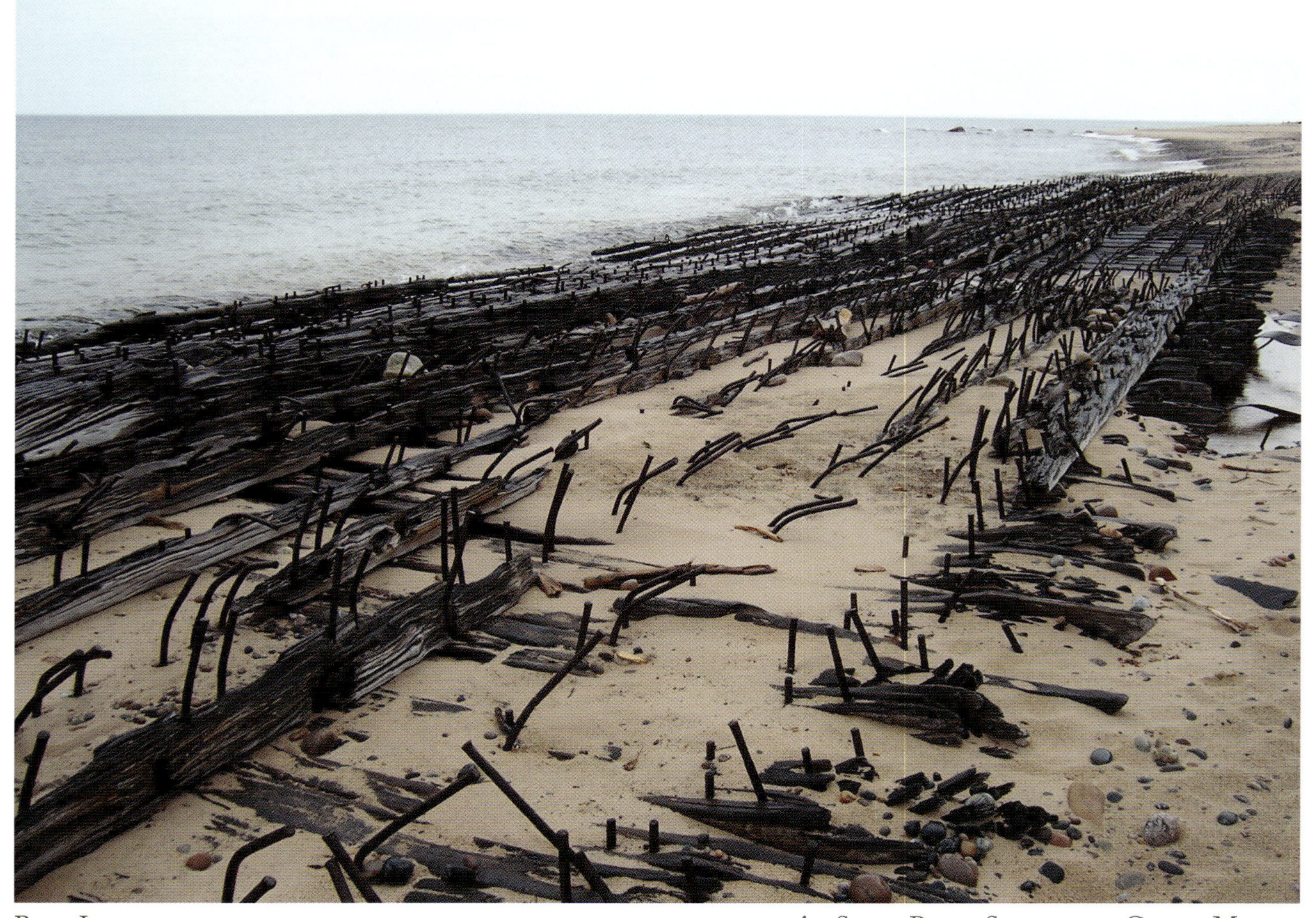

Barb Jenkins

Au Sable Point Shipwreck, Grand Marais

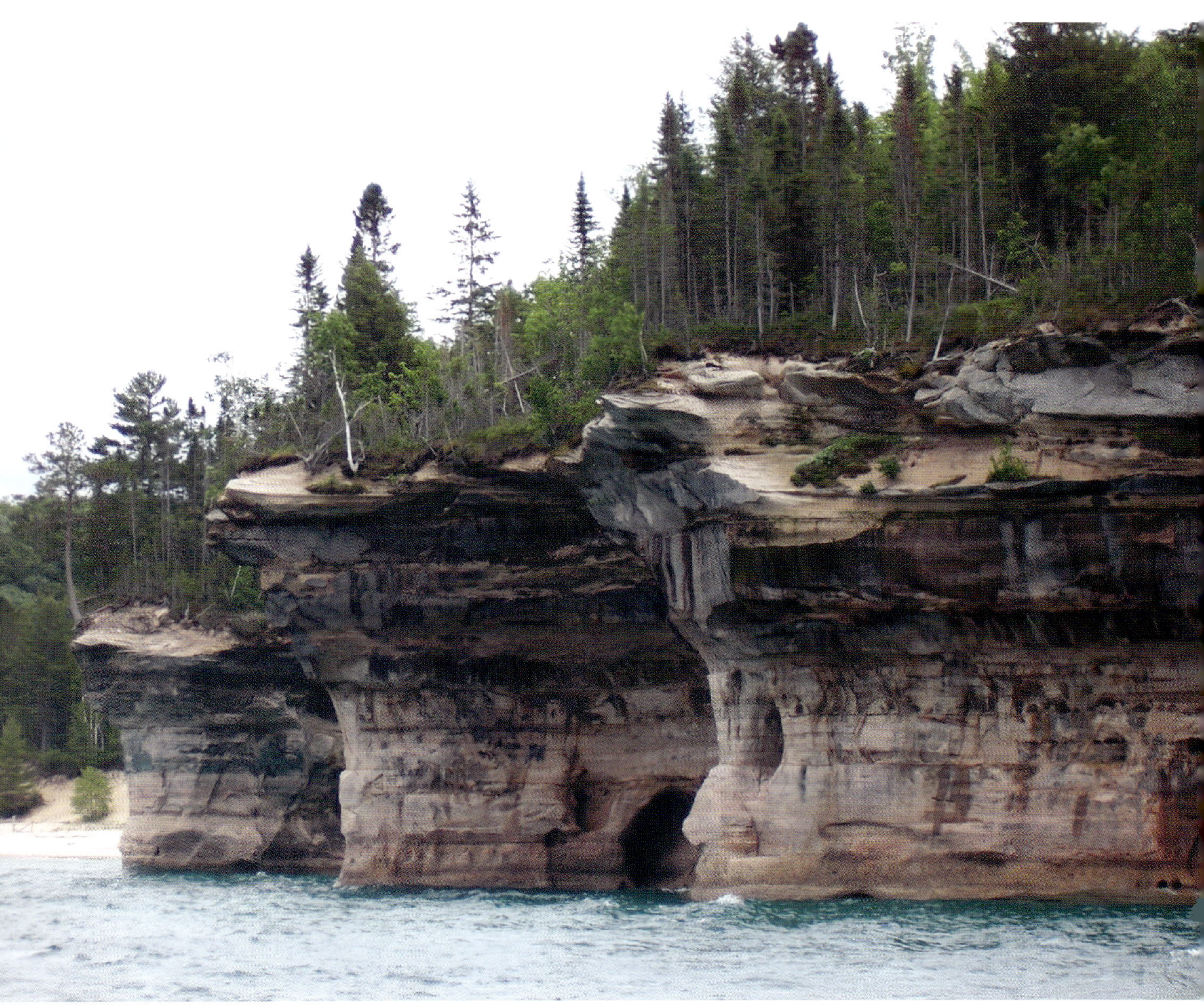

Barb Jenkins

Battleship Row, Pictured Rocks National Lakeshore

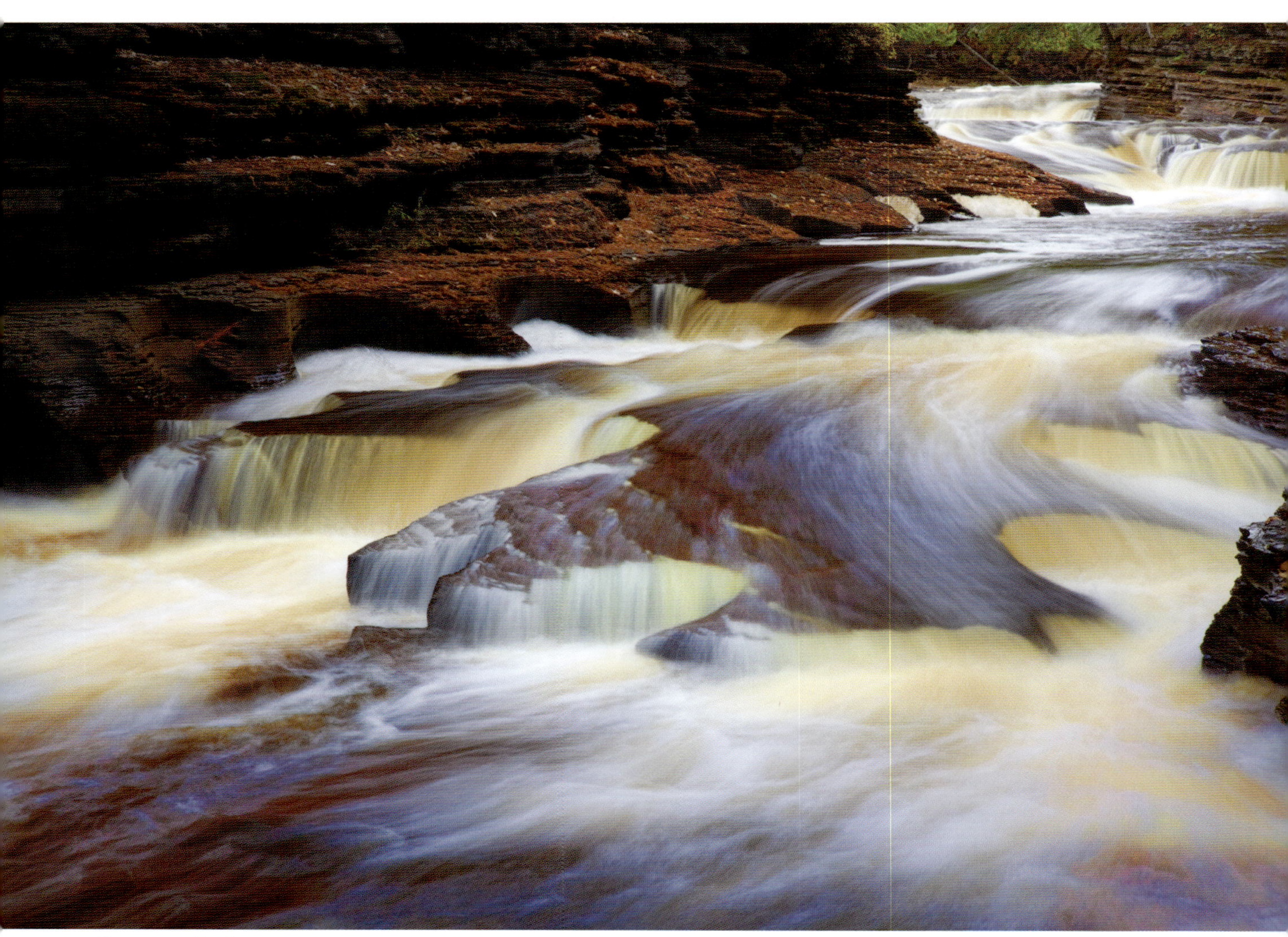

Stephen R. Sage

Presque Isle Falls, Porcupine Mountains Wilderness State Park

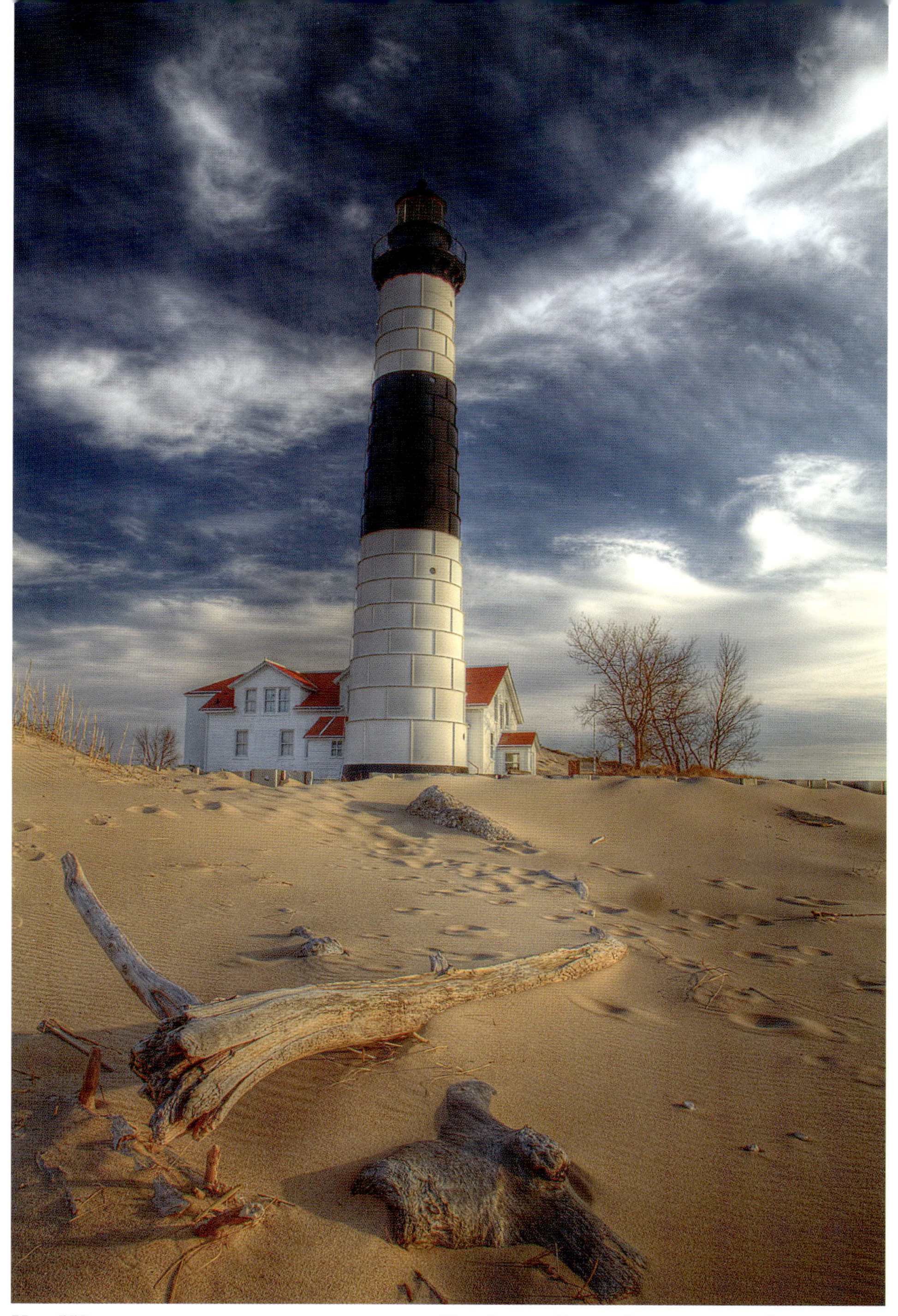

Kim Wilcox Big Sable Point Lighthouse, Ludington

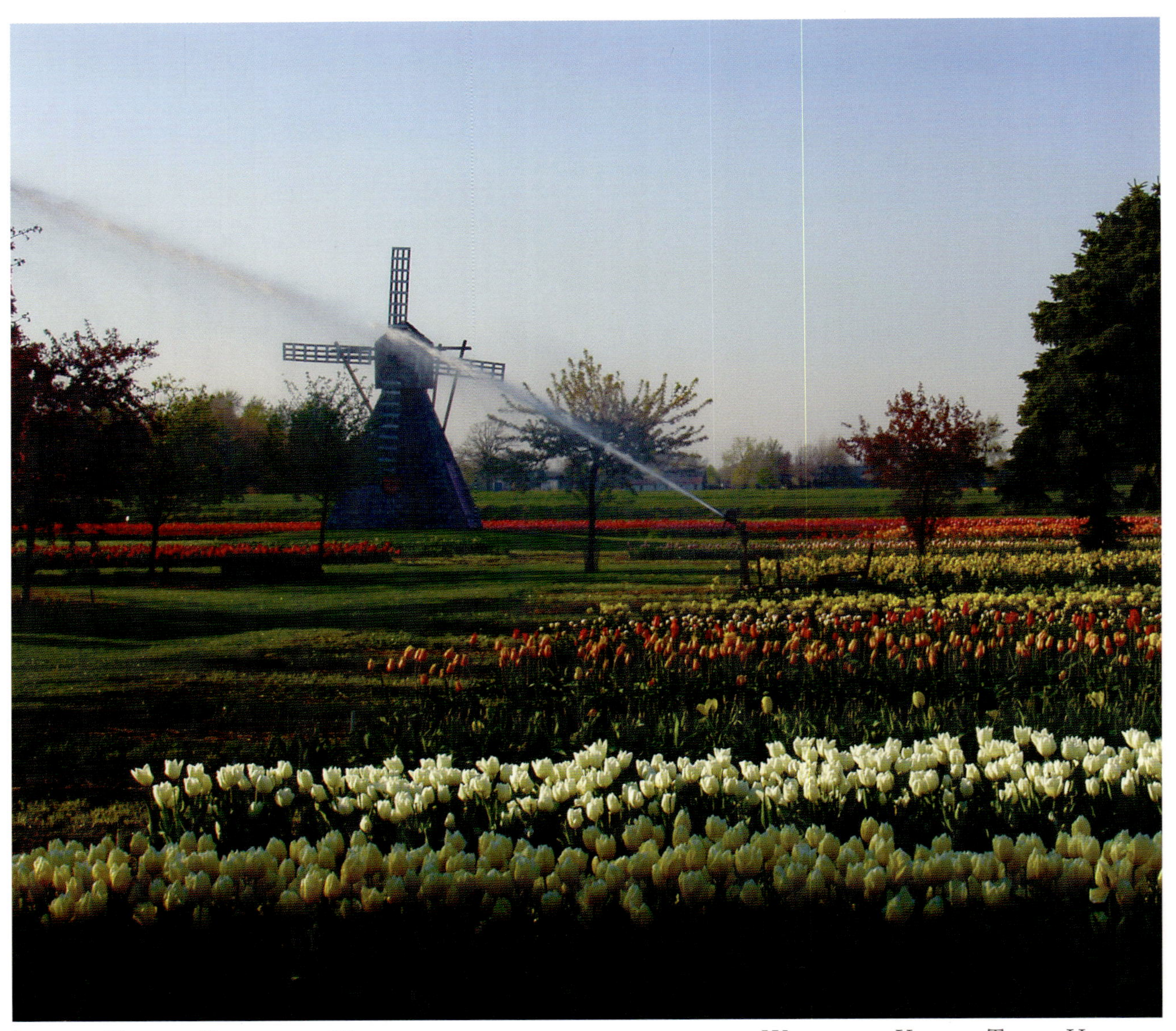

Jack van Heest & Valerie van Heest — Windmill & Veldeer Tulips, Holland

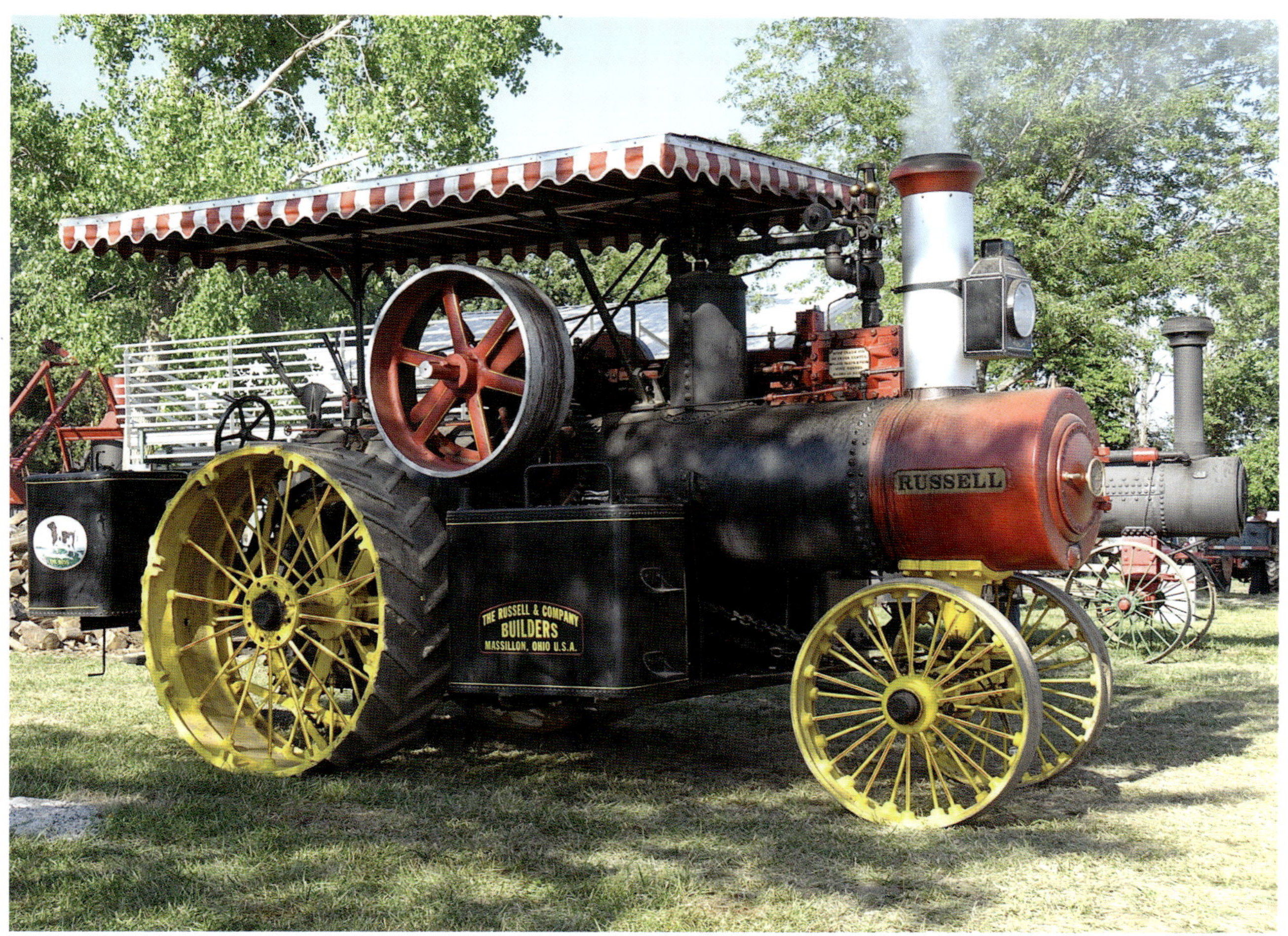

Loren S. Shattuck — Tractor, Michigan Steam Engine & Threshers Club Reunion, Mason

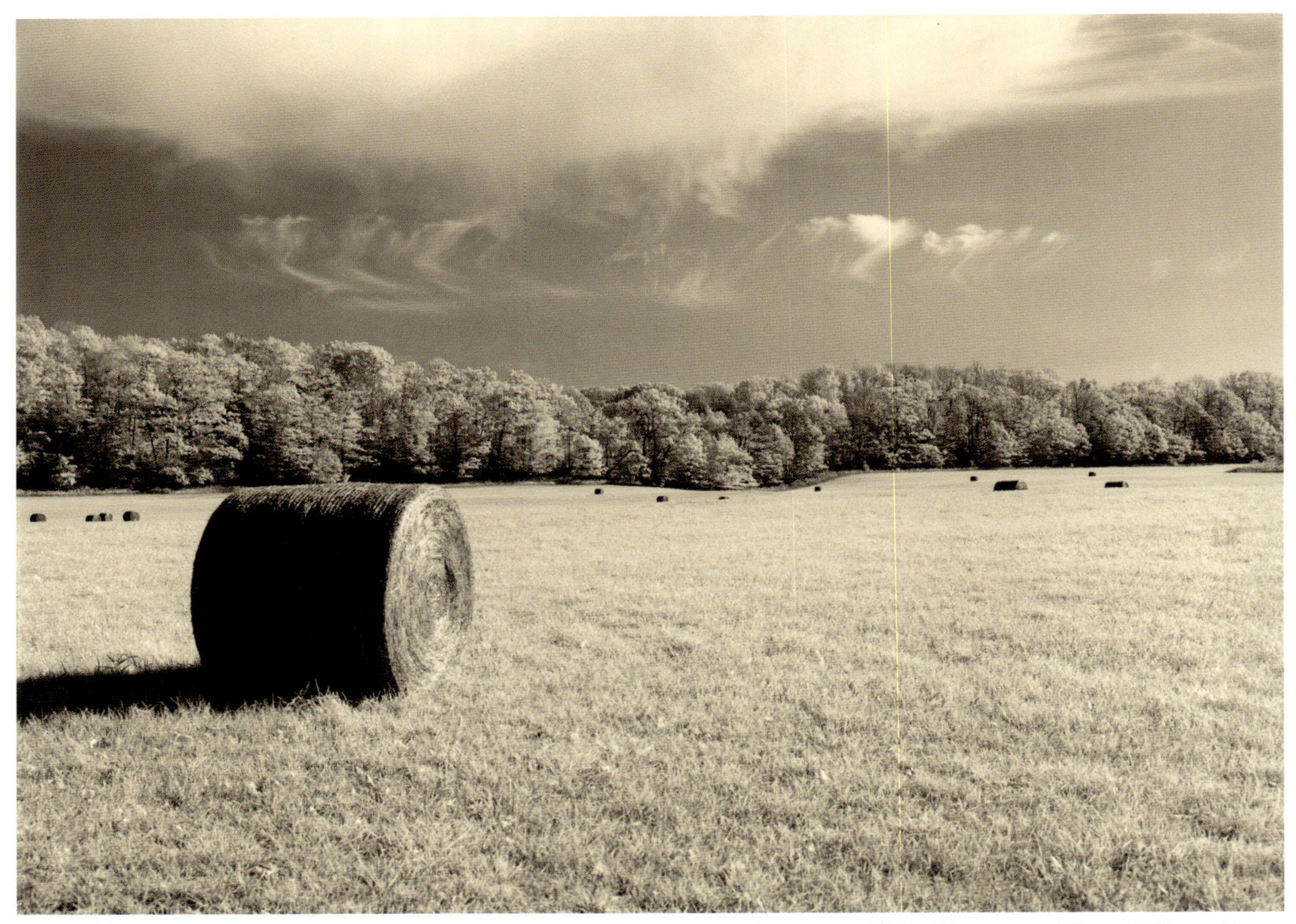

Scott Nicholson

Along 119 "The Tunnel of Trees," Good Hart

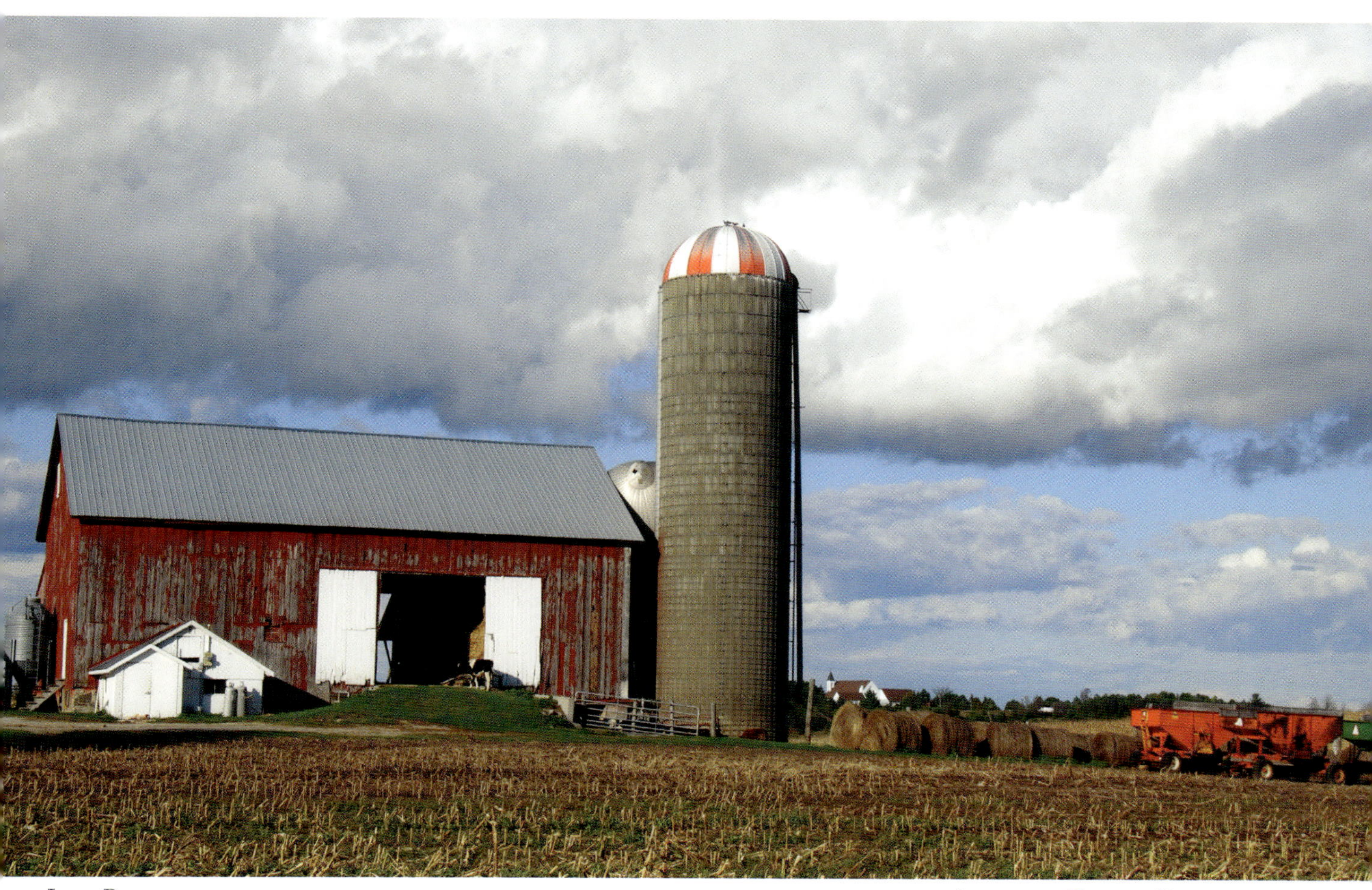

Jessi Bjorkman

American Dream, Petoskey

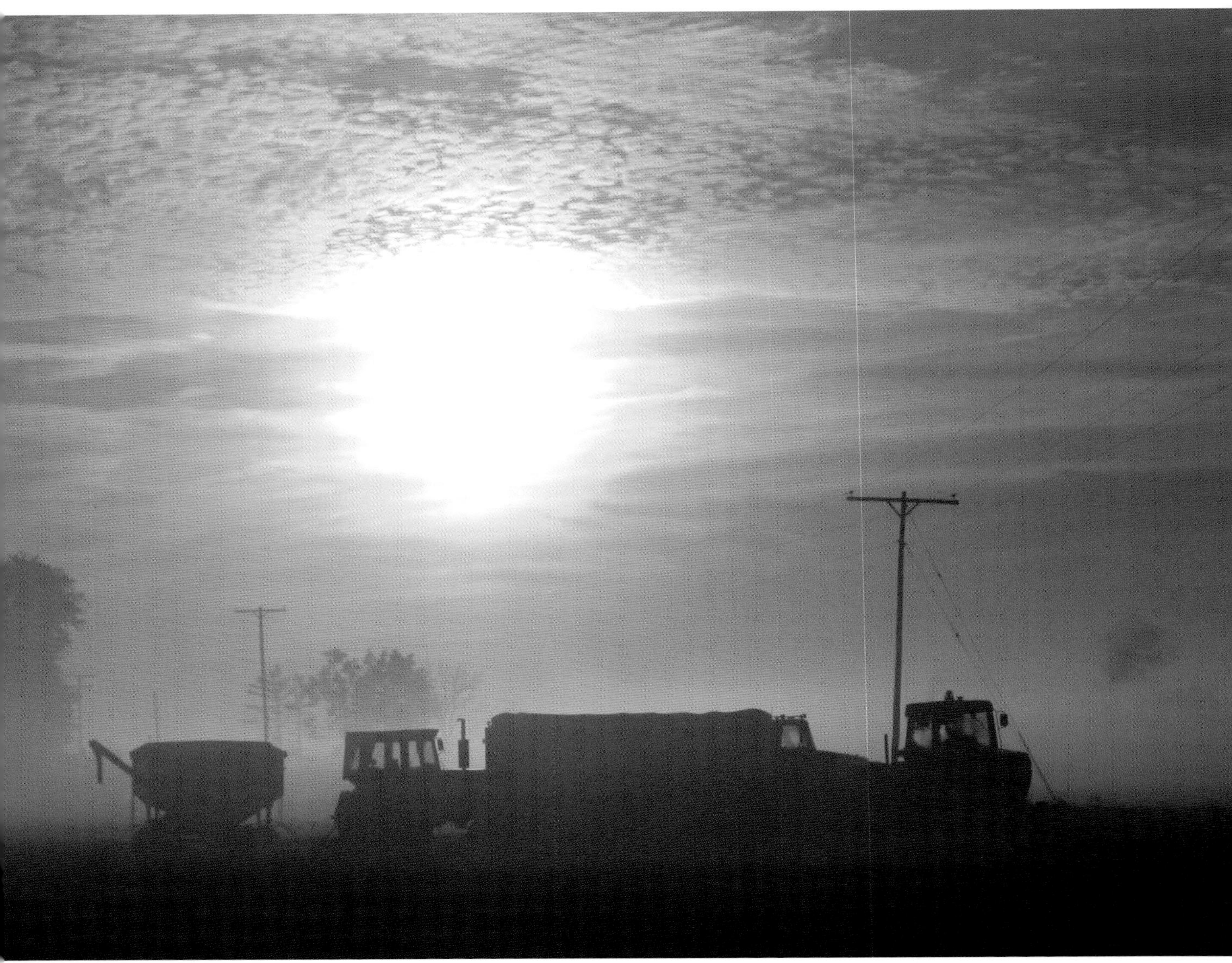

Ron Berby

Foggy Start of Bean-Field Harvest, Alaiedon Township

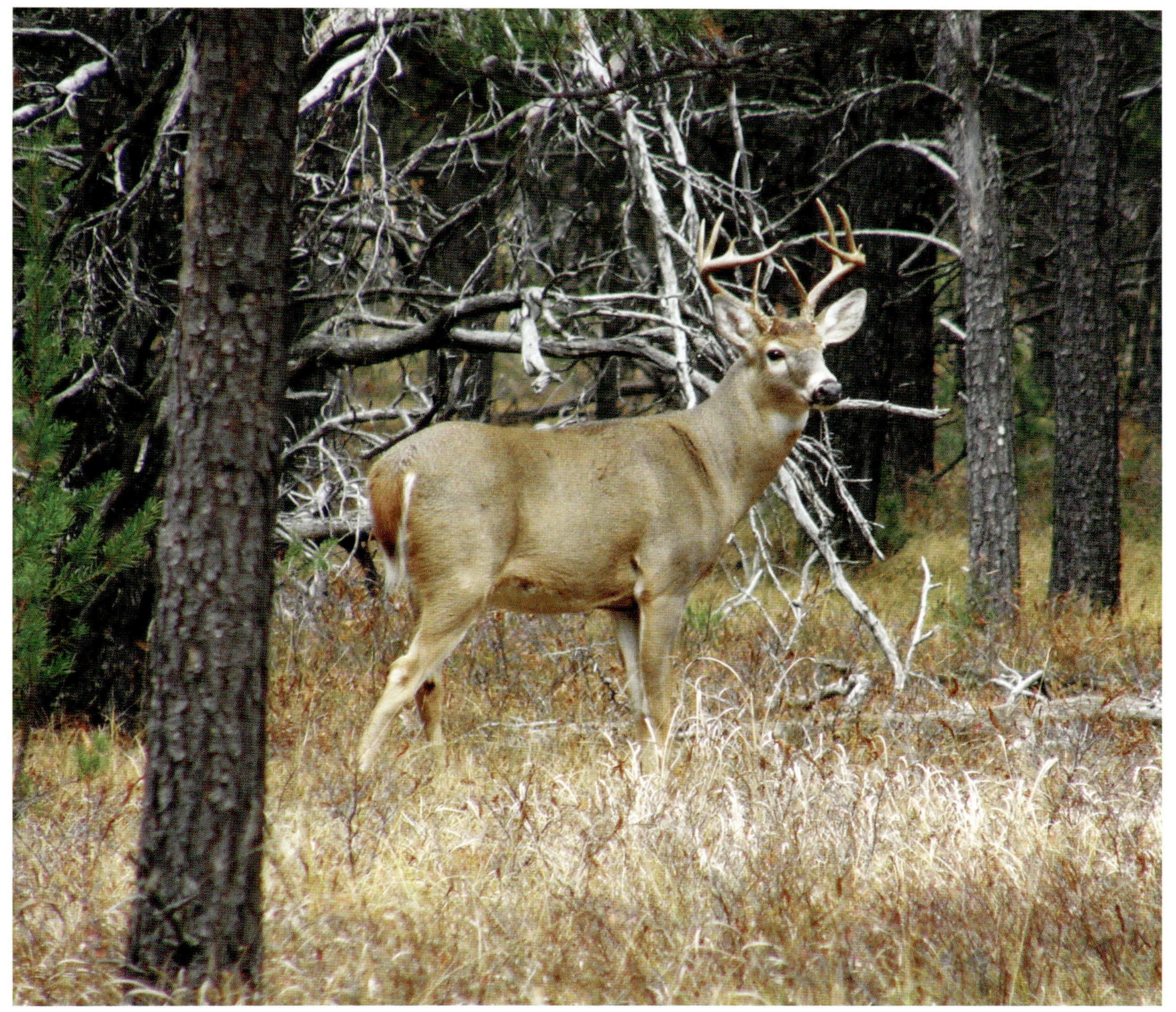

Marion J. Wood

Buck, Atlanta

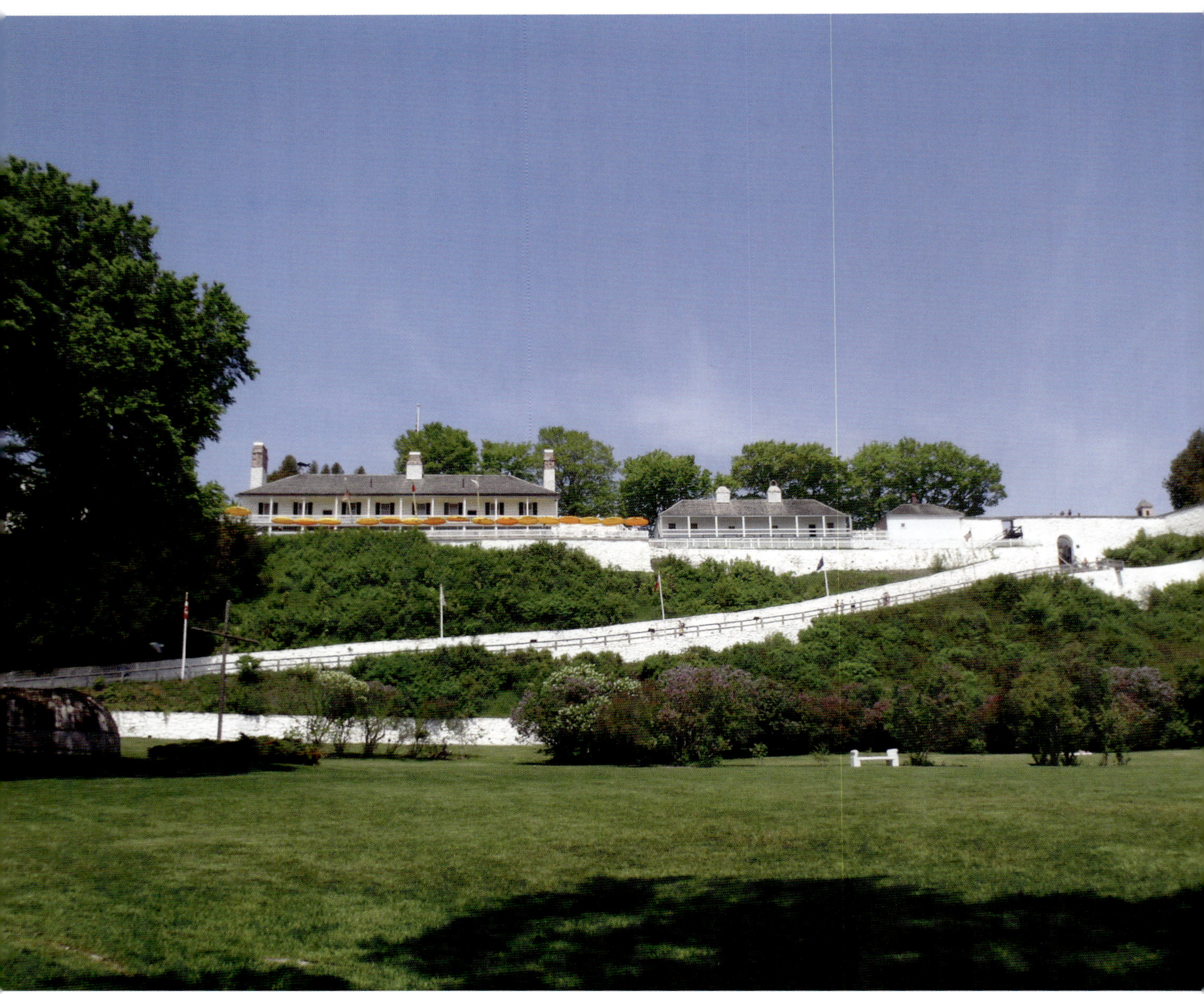

Julie Taylor

Fort Mackinac, Mackinac Island

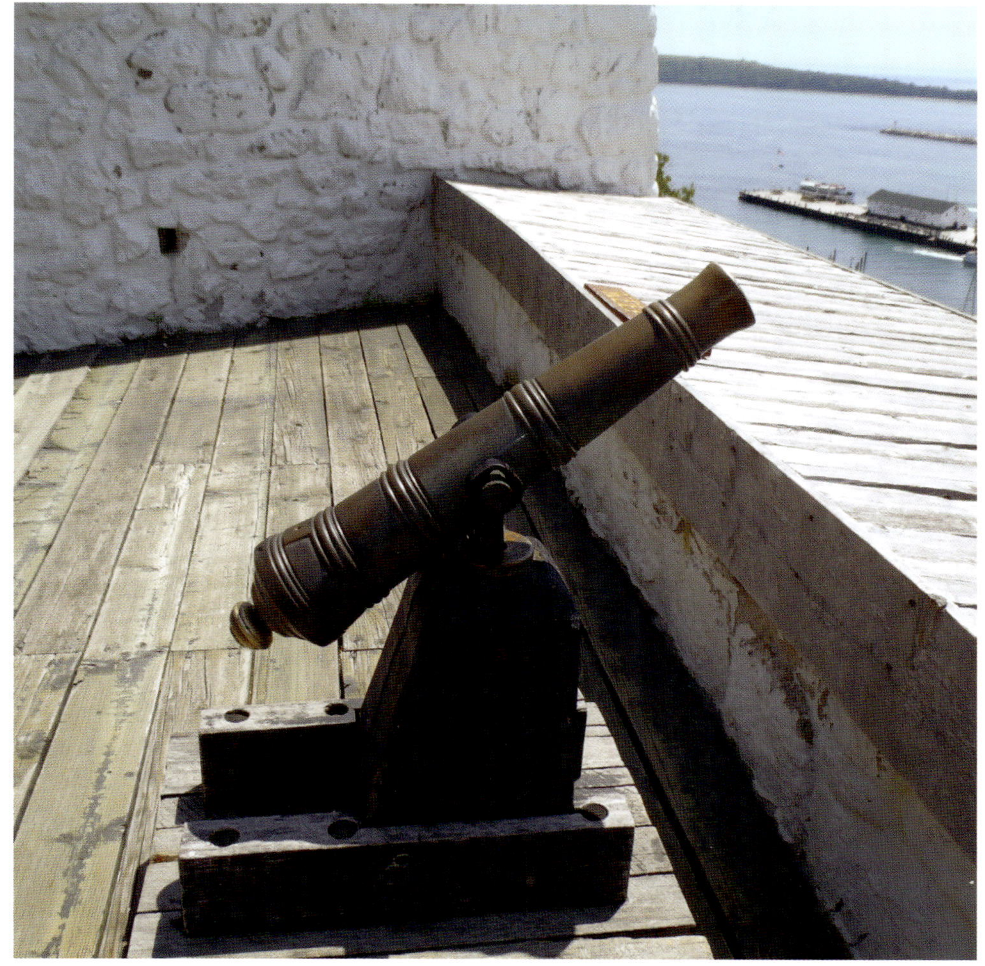

Julie Taylor — Fort Mackinac Cannon, Mackinac Island

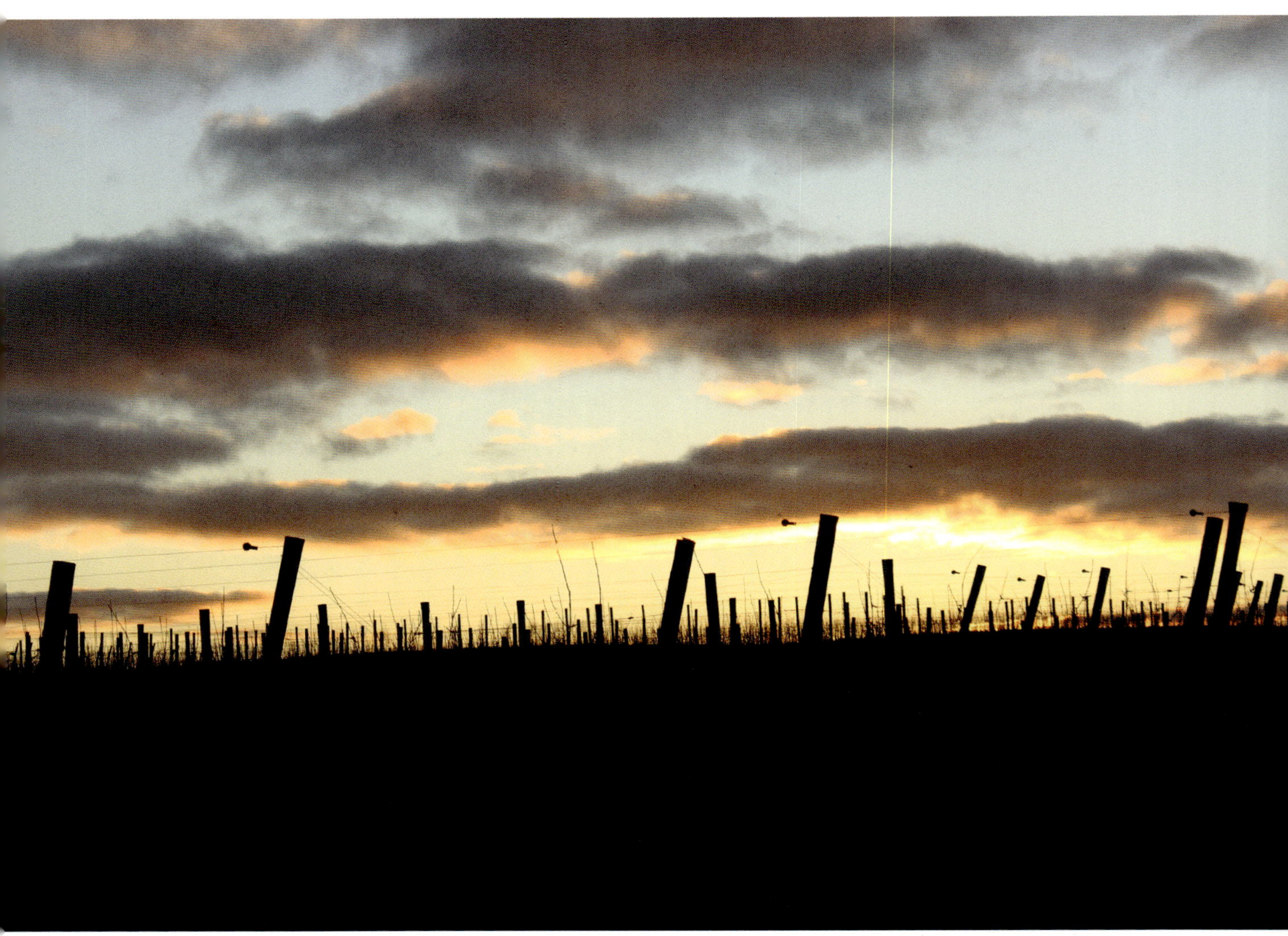

Jacquelyn Dawson

Country Sunset, Kent City

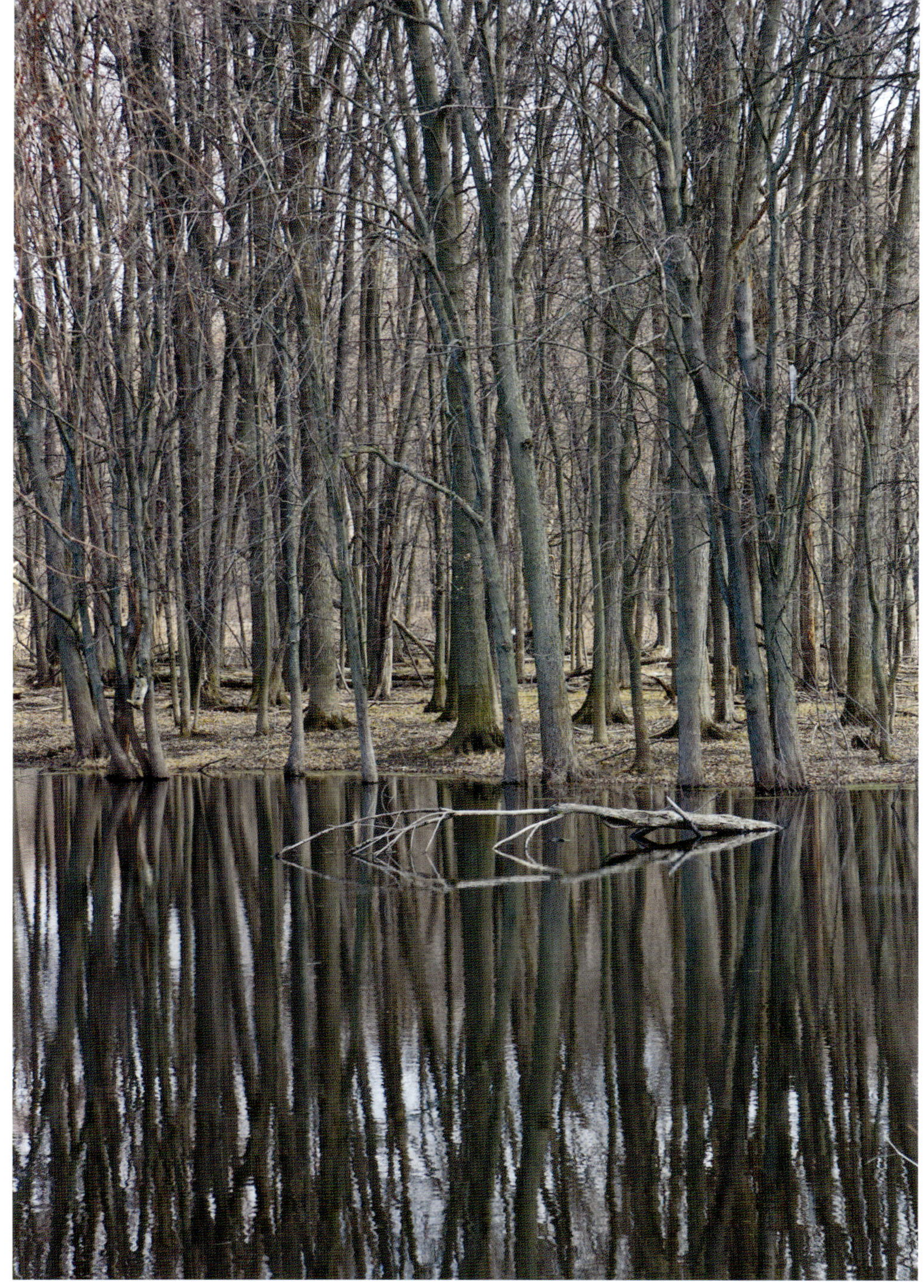

Cyndy Williams Tree Reflection, Shiawassee National Wildlife Refuge

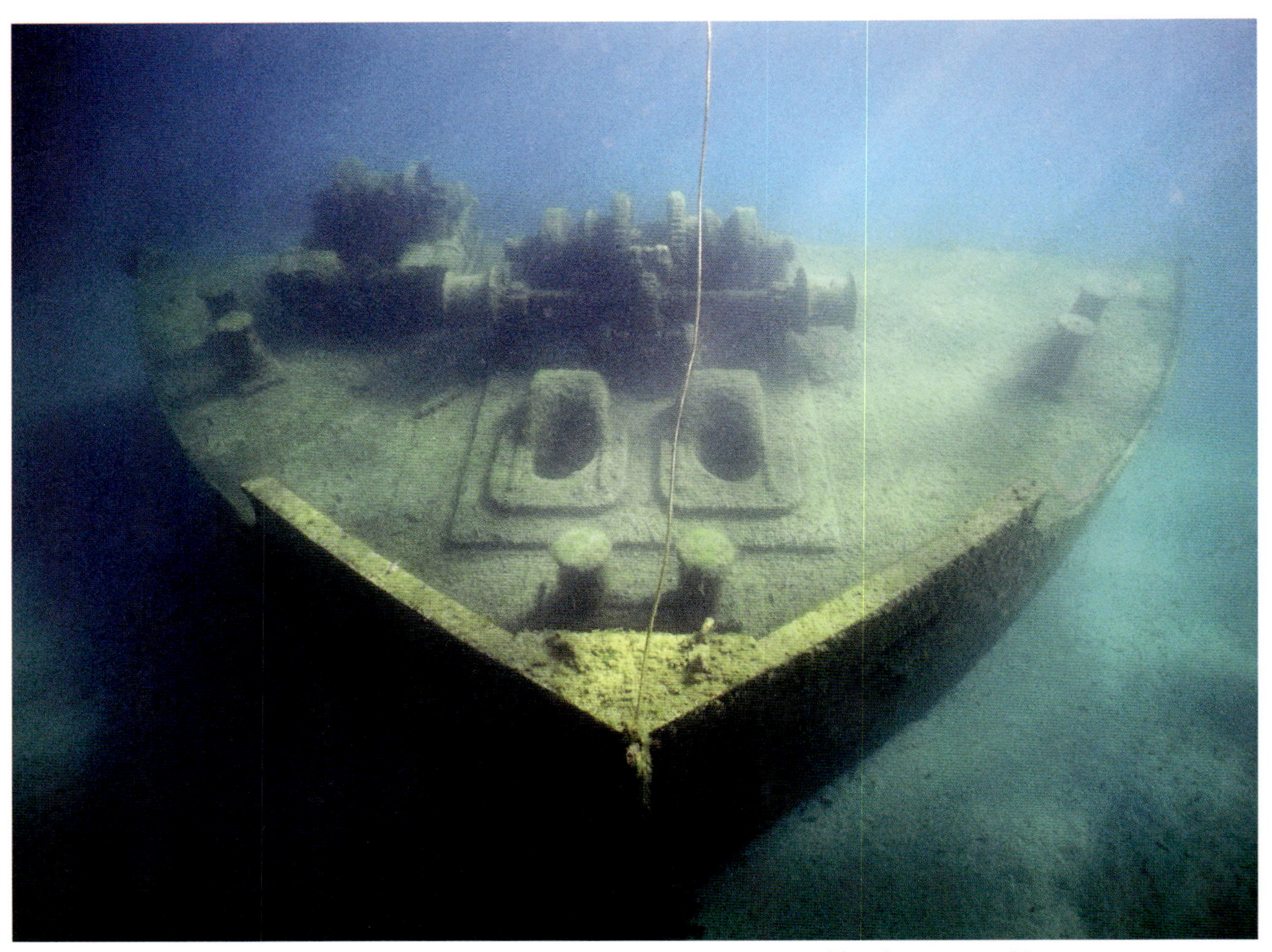

Valerie van Heest

Ghost of the Oceana Coast: The Shipwreck Novadoc lost in 1940 off of the Silver Lake Dunes, near Pentwater

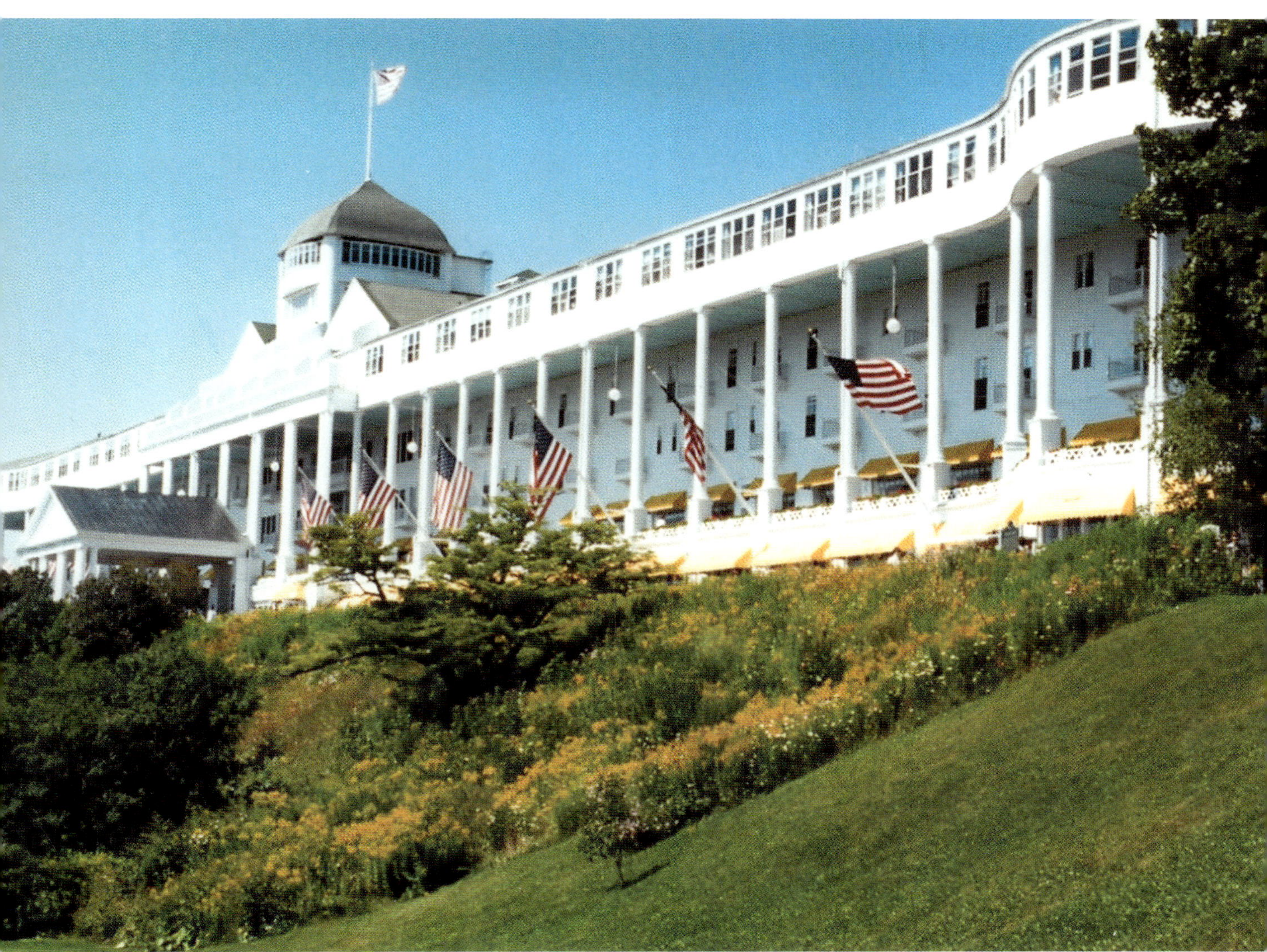

Loren S. Shattuck — Grand Hotel, Mackinac Island

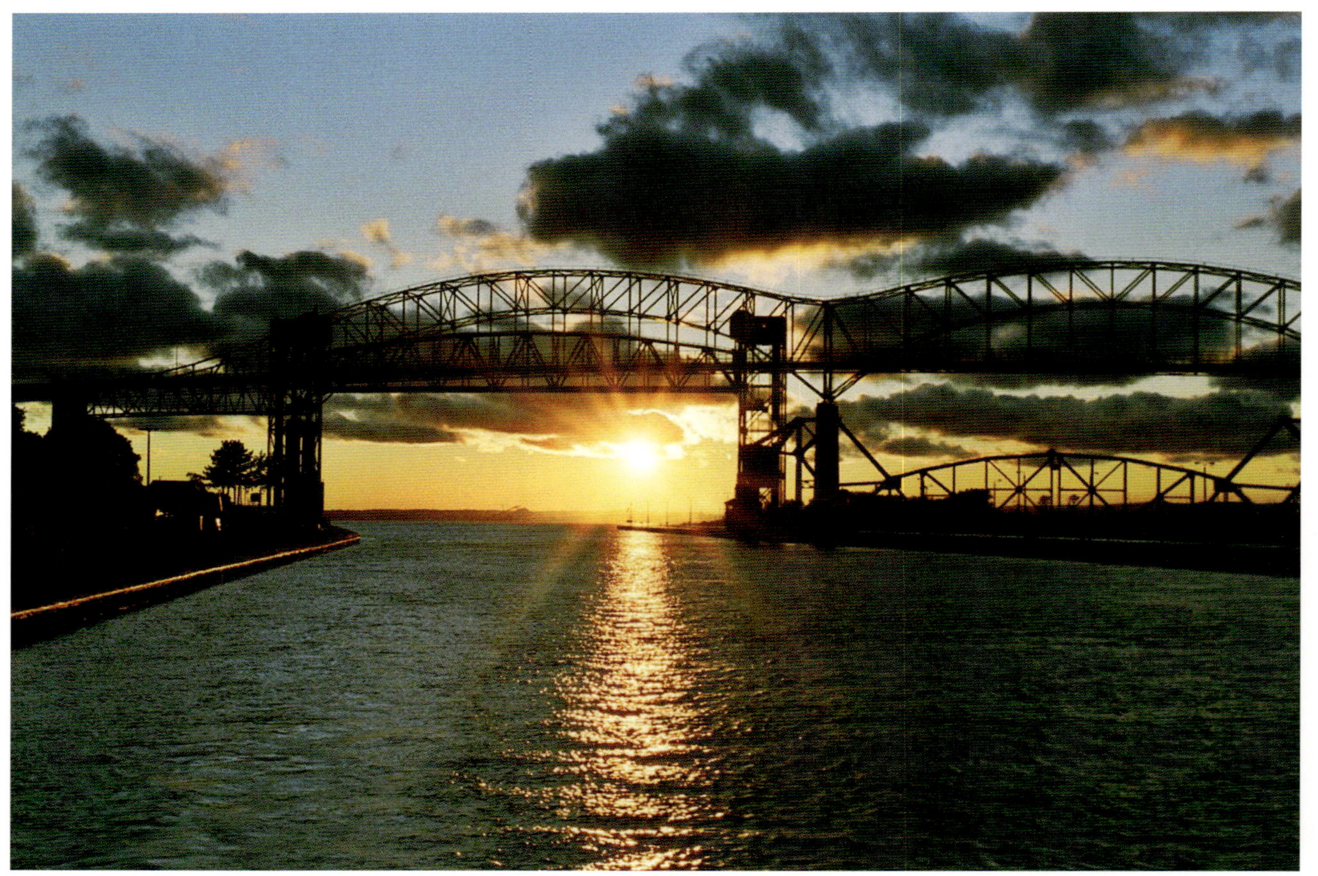

Caitlin Sullivan — International Sunset, Sault Locks, Sault Sainte Marie

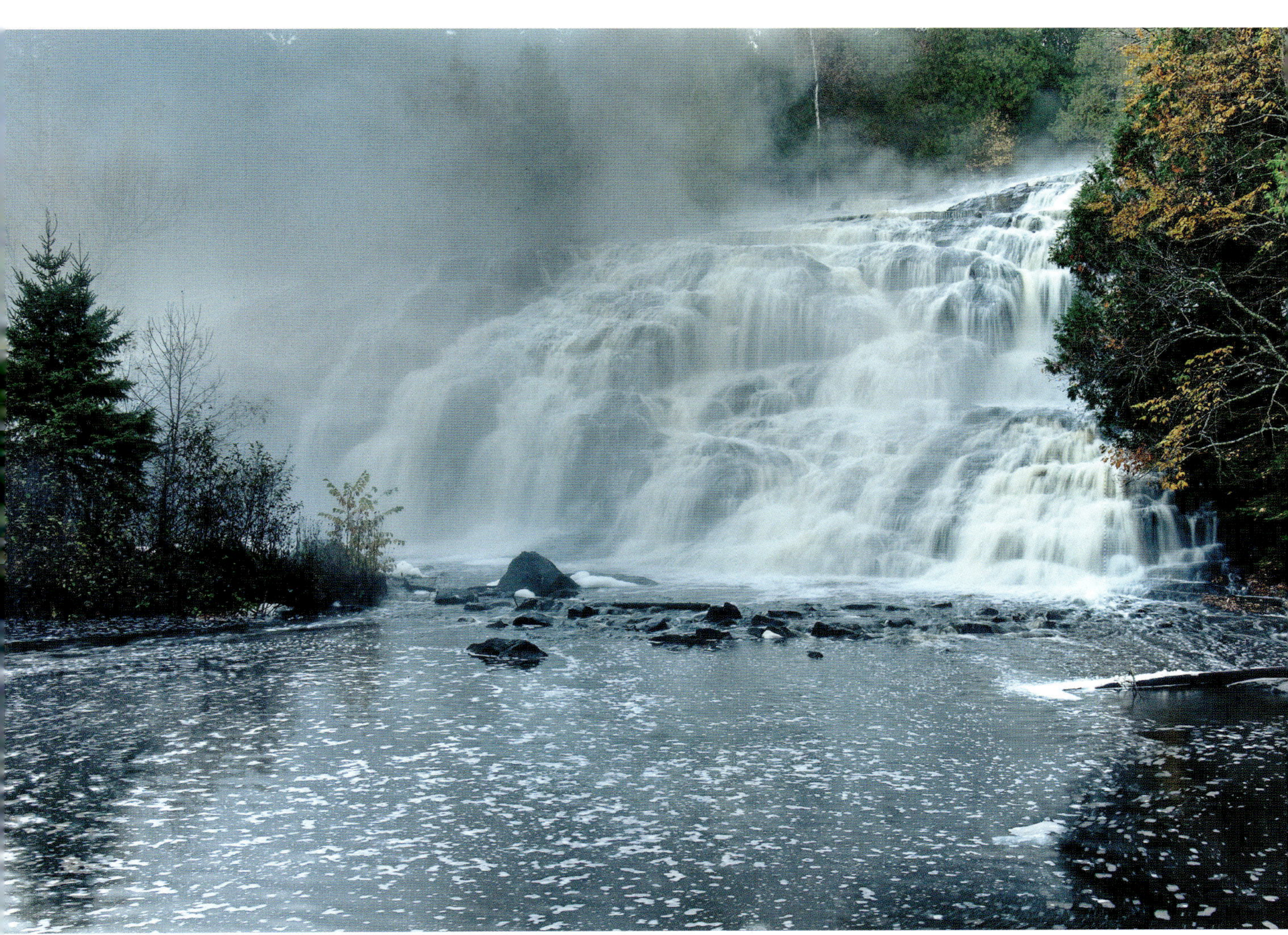

Alan L. Jones

Morning at Bond Falls, Middle Branch of the Ontonagon River

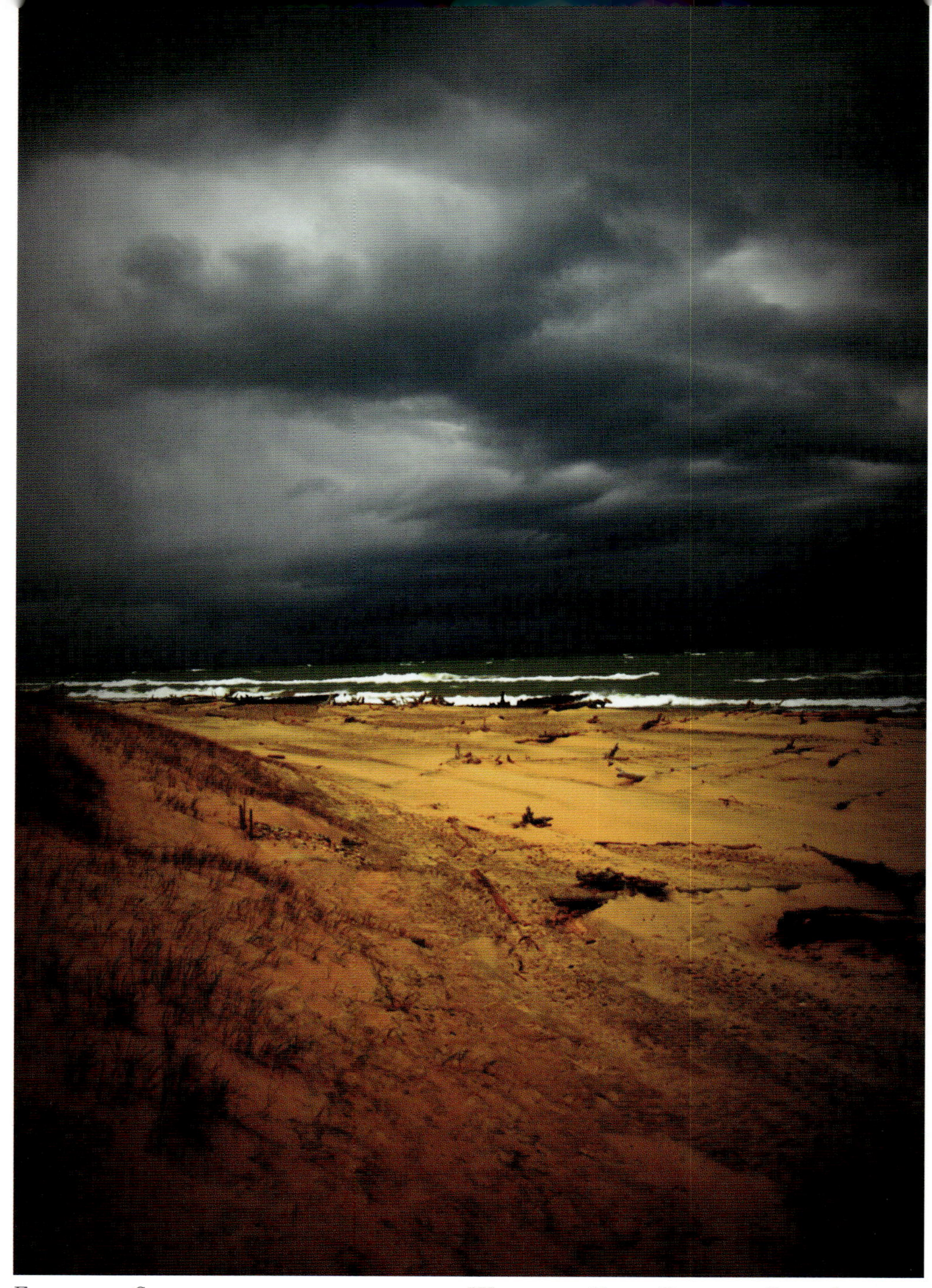

Elizabeth Smith Whitefish Point Beach on Lake Superior

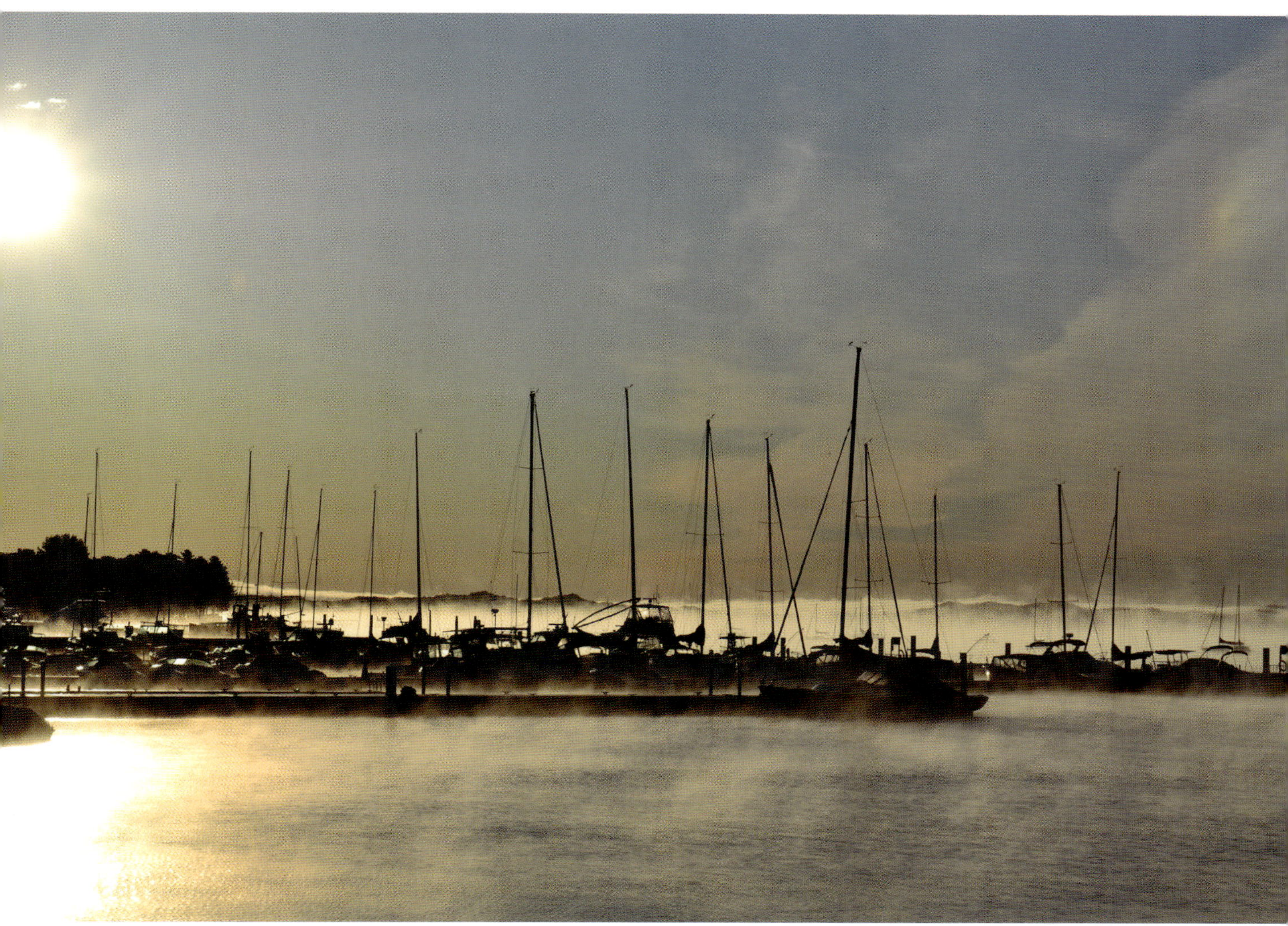

Brandy L. Crump

Sunrise on Little Traverse Bay, Harbor Springs

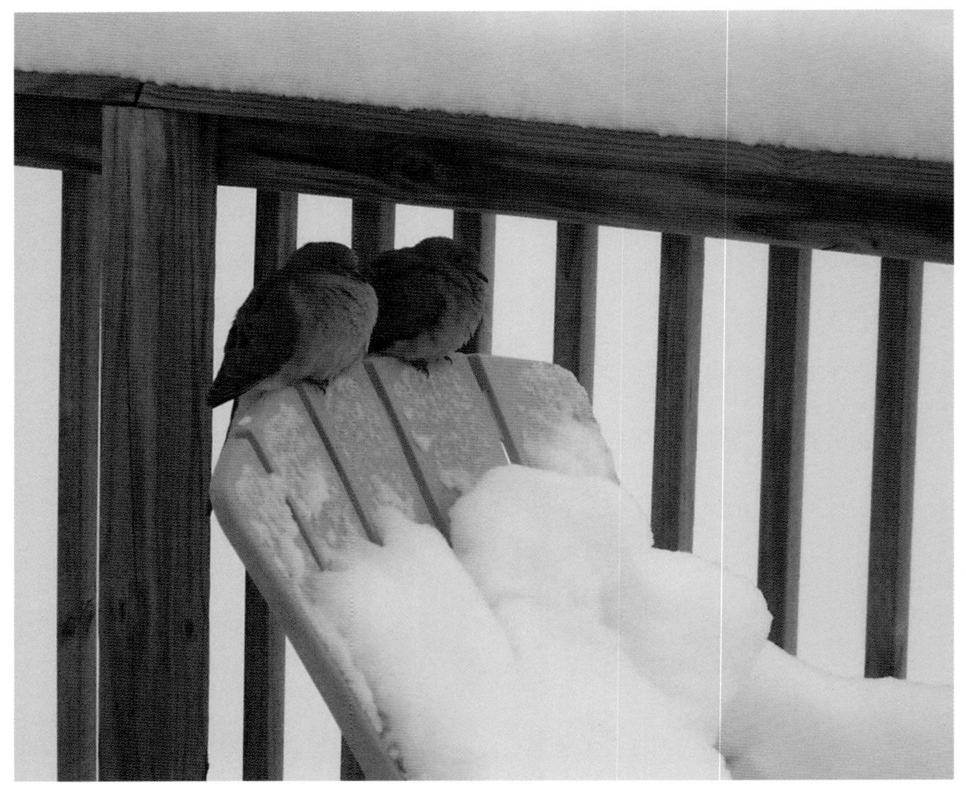

Barb Jenkins — Snowbirds on Chair, Caledonia

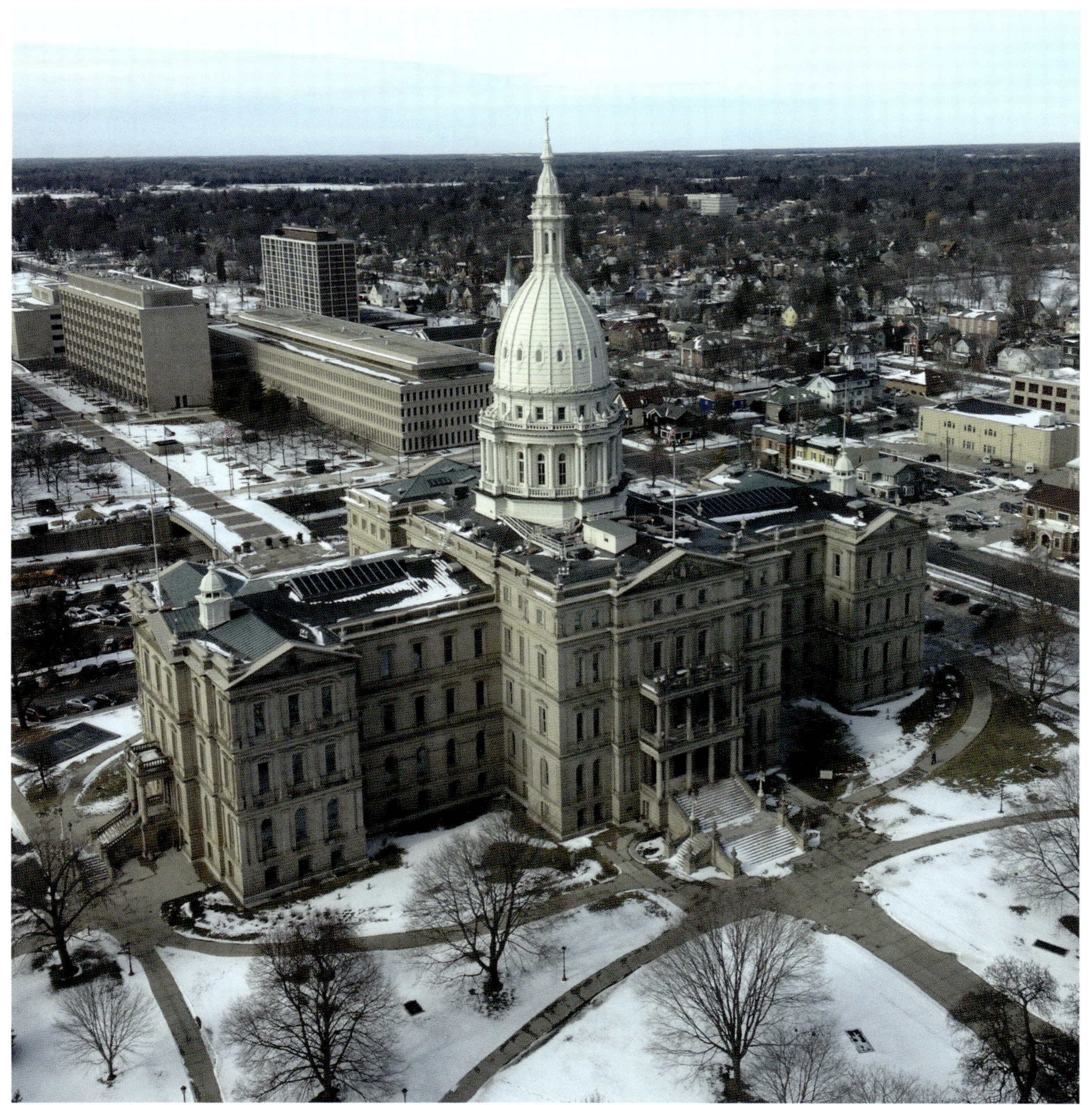

William Mayes

Where It Happens, Lansing

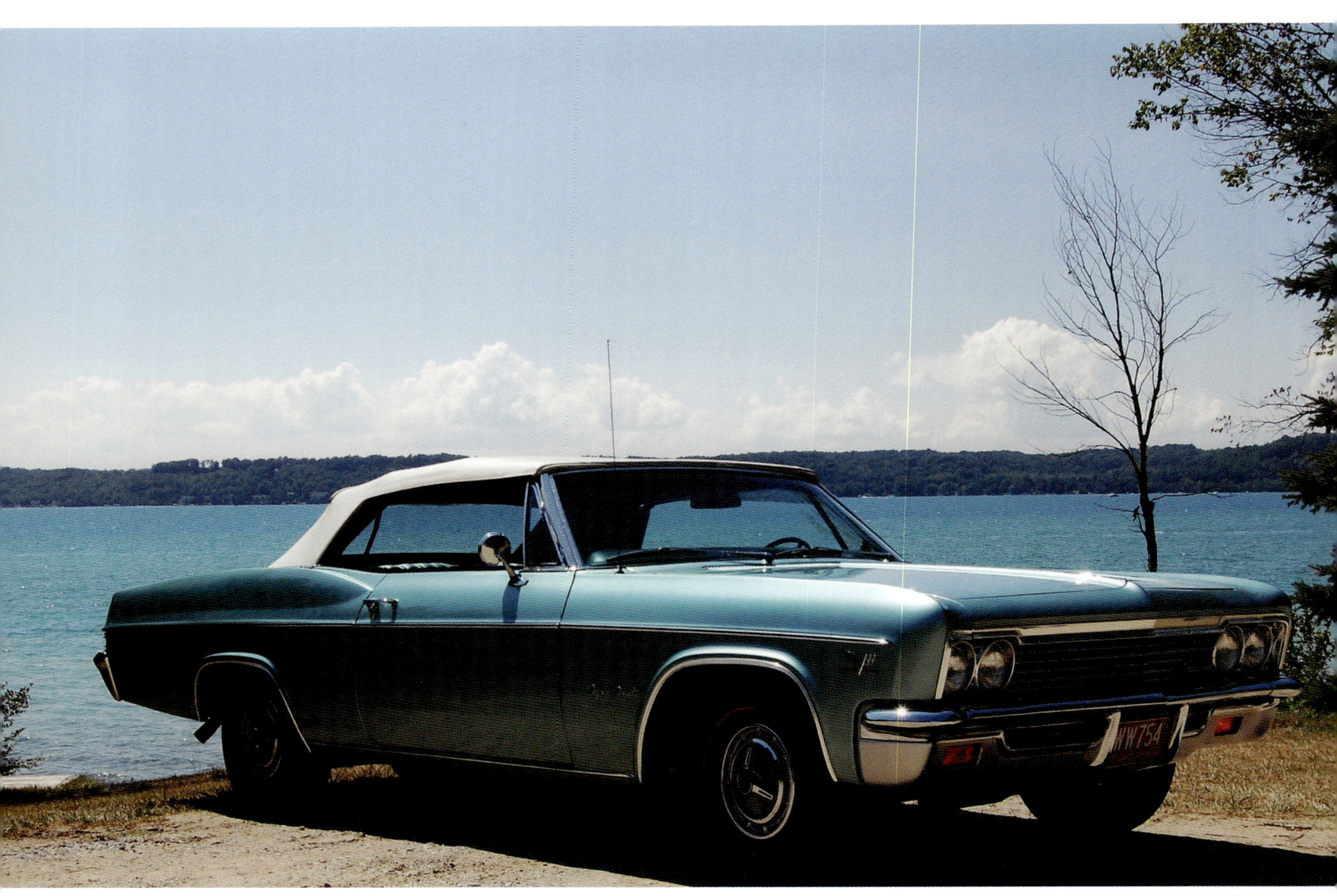

Christina Fischbach

1966 Chevrolet Impala SS Convertible, Torch Lake

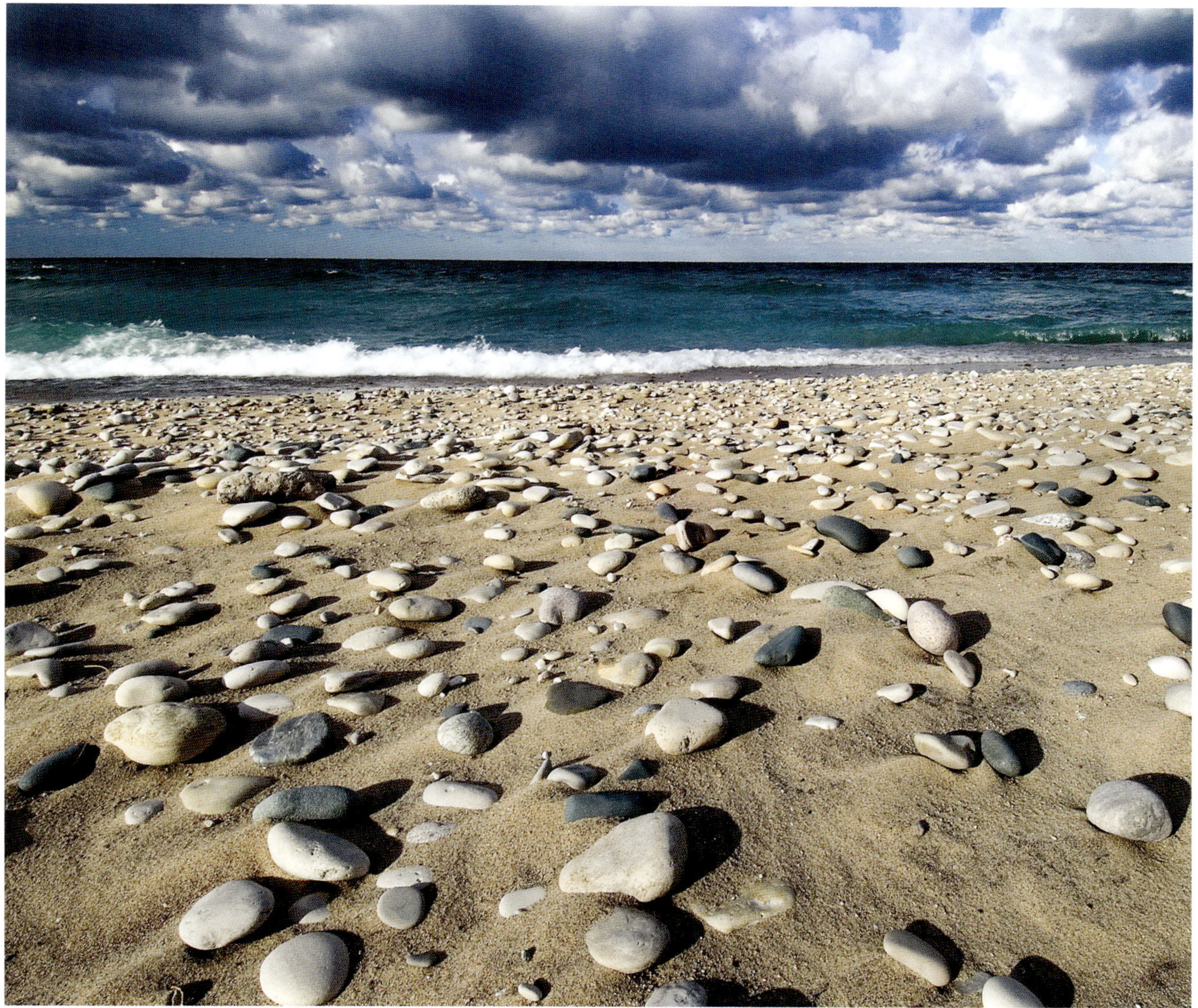

Tom Haxby

Stoney Beach, Point Betsie Lighthouse Beach

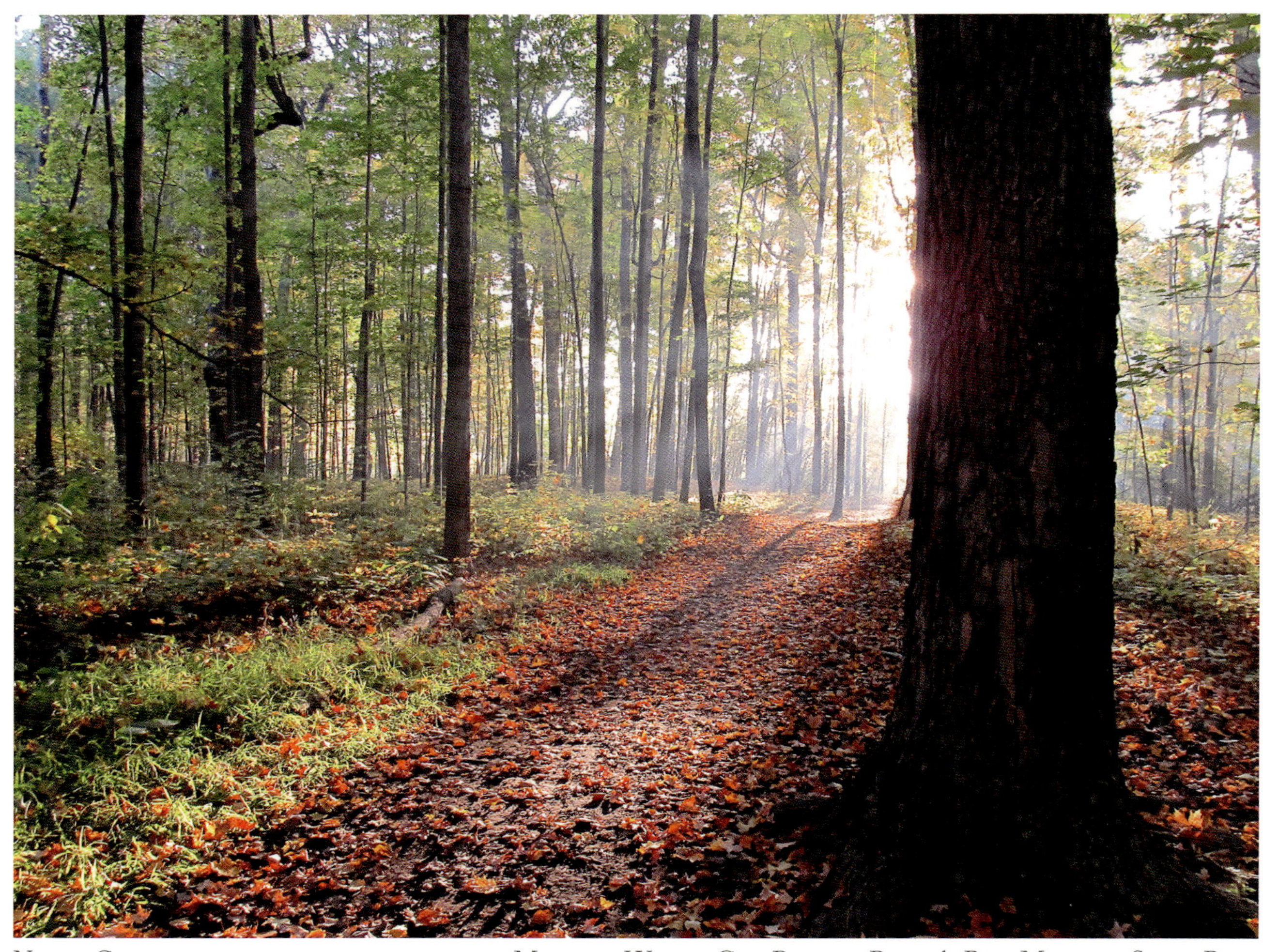

Nancy Cassel — Morning Walk—God Playing Peek-A-Boo, Maybury State Park

Hoary Puccoon

Joyce Benvenuto

Like a dune flower or birch tree in a row
(none the same) I have become Michigan.
As a child, I dreamed of Indians: I was one
of a long canoe on St. Ignace gull-tracked water.
I grew. My vision never changed. I have become
an Indian, of sorts, a child of many fish, more than fleas
on a dog; and sun; a child impervious to cold
and never lost; a child with waiting feet
like rested cats and eyes that wait, their lid-
sheaths not entirely closed, et cetera. You see,
Michigan has made me an original inhabitant.
Thus, when I am dead my obituary can be read by few
                    not print at all but bark
configurations on the page, readable only by those
becoming Michigan themselves. They will note
the death—Hoary Puccoon—and place her
                    in dune memory.

For those of you who do not believe,
look at any obituary section. You will see:
It is not all print of time, of place,
bereaved by whom, services at, donations to…
Here and there, startling breaks in the print column,
the words—not words, but wounds, knots, lines in bark:
birch-print of others like myself…
                    Place is the Grand River shore.
                    Time—absurd
                    only the temperature can change.
                    Form slips from bark to wave,
                    throws in the line, and Michigan
                    gives, and feeds and gives.

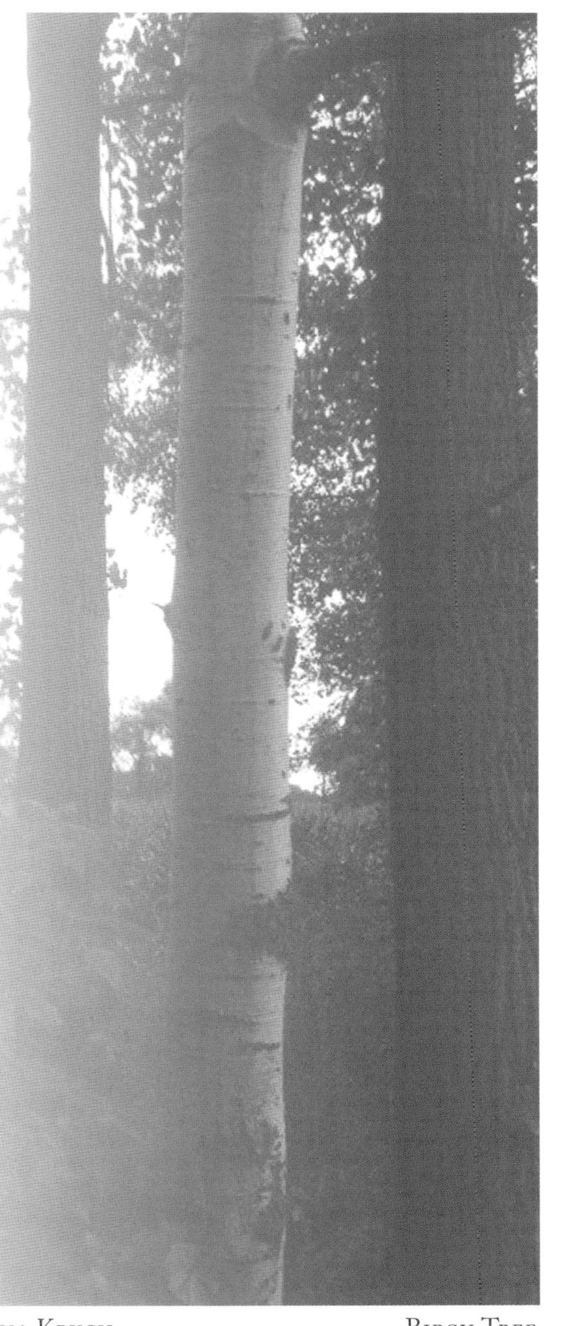

Mary Anna Kruch   Birch Tree

INDEX OF PHOTOGRAPHERS

INDEX OF LOCATIONS

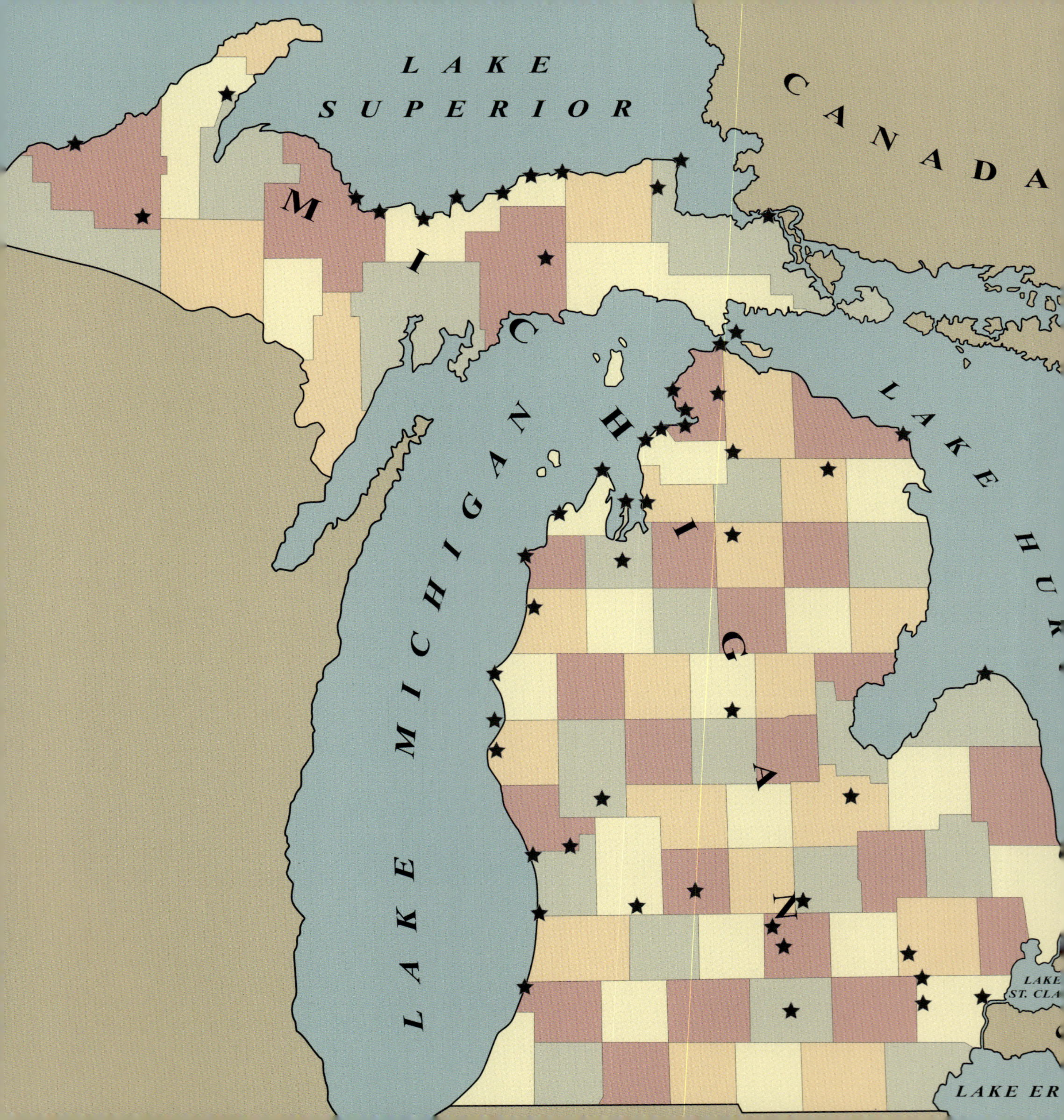

LAKE SUPERIOR
CANADA
MICHIGAN
LAKE MICHIGAN